# A Guide to the
# Dyfi Valley Way

## Laurence Main

WESTERN MAIL & ECHO LTD

# Acknowledgements

Great care has been taken to be accurate. The publishers cannot, however, accept responsibility for any errors which may appear, or their consequences.

Most of these routes are believed to be Rights of Way. However, the route over the Arans is at present a courtesy path, as is the access path to the burial mound of the Red Bandits of Mawddwy. Dogs are never welcome on sheep pastures, but take particular heed of the warning notices not to bring them on the Arans. Some forest tracks are used, and on these you walk at your own risk. It is essential that you follow the Country Code. Please remember that you cross private land as a privilege, so do not spoil it for those who may follow you.

Many people helped me whilst working on this book, none more so than Tom Jones of Llanymawddwy, whose knowledge of his valley and his hills was invaluable and inspiring. As I came down from Aran Fawddwy whilst preparing this second edition of this guidebook, I heard that Tom had died the night before. I would like to dedicate this book to his memory.

Copyright ©

Published in Great Britain by Western Mail & Echo Ltd.,
Havelock Street, Cardiff CF1 1XR. 1996

Design and typesetting:  A Jones, C Williams and L Baker
Scanning:                P Mayled and D Adams

Cover photograph:
Overlooking Dinas Mawddwy from Cefn Coch

All photographs by Laurence Main unless otherwise credited:
P.M . - By Phil Martin
K.A.L. - Supplied by King Arthur's Labyrinth
P.D.C. - By Peter Dobson/Celtica
B.L.R. - Supplied by Bala Lake Railway

British Library Cataloguing in Publication Data.
A Catalogue record for this book is available from the British Library.

I.S.B.N. 1 900477 00 9

Printed by Mid Wales Litho, New Inn, Pontypool, Gwent.

# Introduction

The Dyfi Valley is one of the most beautiful in Wales. Traditionally the frontier between North and South Wales, it is where Gwynedd, Powys and Ceredigion meet today. As the river winds the 30 miles from its source to the sea it passes through a surprising variety of scenery, with its tributaries encouraging you to take a wider view from the surrounding ridges and hills.

There is no better way of exploring this area than on foot. The bulk of this guide consists of a strip map at a generous scale, marking in such details as stiles, gates and signposts, while a gradient profile gives an impression of the ups and downs. Information about public transport, accommodation, shops and cafes is included. There are notes on interesting places to visit.

Read the strip map from the bottom to the top of each page (when walking from Aberdyfi to Borth), so that the map faces the direction in which you walk. As this means that north cannot always be at the top of the page, the direction of north is indicated on each page. The numbers of the relevant Ordnance Survey maps are also given, so that the strip map can be related to the surrounding countryside.

There are nine sections, suggesting that the Dyfi Valley Way makes an ideal backpacking holiday for a week and a second weekend. It is just as enjoyable, however, when split into short sections and walked at convenient intervals.

## ORDER OF CONTENT

*'A day's walking; a week's good health.'* *(French proverb)*

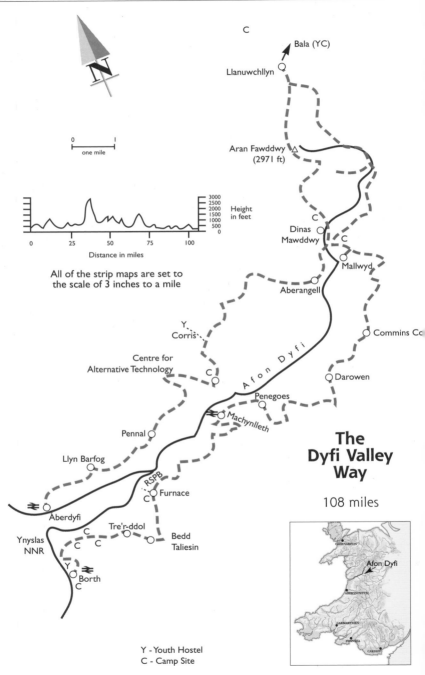

one mile

3000
2500
2000
1500
1000
500
0

Height in feet

0    25    50    75    100

Distance in miles

All of the strip maps are set to
the scale of 3 inches to a mile

C

Bala (YC)

Llanuwchllyn

Aran Fawddwy
(2971 ft)

C

Dinas
Mawddwy

C

Mallwyd

Aberangell

Y
Corris

Commins Co

Centre for
Alternative Technology

C

A f o n   D y f i

Darowen

Penegoes

Pennal

Machynlleth

Llyn Barfog

**The
Dyfi Valley
Way**

108 miles

RSPB

Furnace
C

Aberdyfi

Tre'r-ddol

Ynyslas
NNR

C      C

Bedd
Taliesin

Y

Borth
C

Afon Dyfi

Y - Youth Hostel
C - Camp Site

*iii*

# Mileage and Facilities Chart

| PLACE | Page | Mile | Train | Bus | Campsite | Youth Hostel | B&B | Shop | Cafe | Post Office | Bank | Launderette | Early Closing Day |
|---|---|---|---|---|---|---|---|---|---|---|---|---|---|
| Aberdyfi | 3 | 0 | ✓ | ✓ | | | ✓ | ✓ | ✓ | ✓ | ✓ | ✓ | W |
| Pennal | 9 | 8 | | ✓ | | | ✓ | ✓ | | ✓ | | | W |
| Pantperthog | 12 | 16 | | ✓ | ✓ | | | | ✓ | | | | |
| Corris | 14 | 19 | | ✓ | | ✓ | ✓ | ✓ | ✓ | ✓ | | | W |
| Aberllefenni | 15 | 21 | | ✓ | | | | | | | | | |
| Aberangell | 18 | 27 | | ✓ | | | | ✓ | | ✓ | | | |
| Dinas Mawddwy | 22 | 31 | | ✓ | ✓ | | ✓ | ✓ | ✓ | ✓ | | | W |
| Llanuwchllyn | 35 | 43 | ✓ | ✓ | ✓ | B | ✓ | ✓ | B | ✓ | B | | W |
| Dinas Mawddwy | 46 | 61 | | ✓ | ✓ | | ✓ | ✓ | ✓ | ✓ | | | W |
| Mallwyd | 49 | 63 | | ✓ | | | ✓ | ✓ | ✓ | ✓ | | | |
| Gwalia | 56 | 74 | | C | | | ✓ | | | | | | |
| Commins Coch | 56 | 75 | | ✓ | | | | ✓ | | ✓ | | | T |
| Cefncoch-Uchaf | 56 | 76 | | R | | | ✓ | R | | R | | | W |
| Darowen | 57 | 77 | | ✓ | ✓ | | ✓ | | | | | | |
| Penegoes | 63 | 85 | | ✓ | | | | | ✓ | ✓ | | | |
| Machynlleth | 65 | 87 | ✓ | ✓ | | | ✓ | ✓ | ✓ | ✓ | ✓ | ✓ | T |
| Eglwys Fach | 69 | 96 | | ✓ | | | ✓ | | | | | | |
| Furnace | 70 | 96 | | ✓ | ✓ | | | ✓ | ✓ | | | | |
| Tre'r-ddol | 74 | 101 | | ✓ | | | ✓ | ✓ | ✓ | | | | |
| Llancynfelyn | 75 | 103 | | | ✓ | | | | | | | | |
| Borth | 77 | 108 | ✓ | ✓ | ✓ | ✓ | ✓ | ✓ | ✓ | ✓ | ✓ | ✓ | W |

B&B - Bed and breakfast in farmhouse, guest house or hotel
B - Proceed to Bala by train or bus
W - Wednesdays      C - Proceed to Cemmaes for bus
T- - Thursdays      R - Proceed to Cemmaes Road

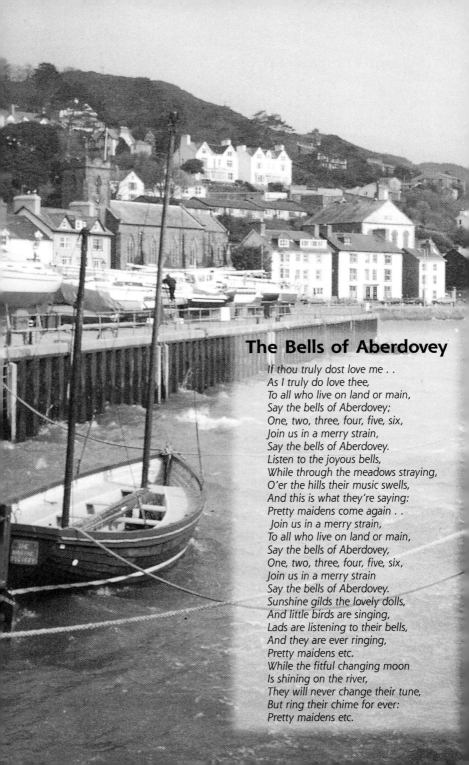

## The Bells of Aberdovey

*If thou truly dost love me . .*
*As I truly do love thee,*
*To all who live on land or main,*
*Say the bells of Aberdovey;*
*One, two, three, four, five, six,*
*Join us in a merry strain,*
*Say the bells of Aberdovey.*
*Listen to the joyous bells,*
*While through the meadows straying,*
*O'er the hills their music swells,*
*And this is what they're saying:*
*Pretty maidens come again . .*
* Join us in a merry strain,*
*To all who live on land or main,*
*Say the bells of Aberdovey,*
*One, two, three, four, five, six,*
*Join us in a merry strain*
*Say the bells of Aberdovey.*
*Sunshine gilds the lovely dolls,*
*And little birds are singing,*
*Lads are listening to their bells,*
*And they are ever ringing,*
*Pretty maidens etc.*
*While the fitful changing moon*
*Is shining on the river,*
*They will never change their tune,*
*But ring their chime for ever:*
*Pretty maidens etc.*

# *Aberdyfi - Pennal*

## Section One (miles 0 - 8¾)

Aberdyfi means the mouth of the Dyfi. This delightful village is situated on a sandy foreshore on the northern side of the Dyfi estuary where the river flows into Cardigan Bay. Charles Dibdin made the village famous when he composed the song *The Bells of Aberdovey* in 1785. It was sung by a comic Welsh character in Dibden's Drury Lane hit *Liberty Hall* and was later associated with Madam Edith Wynne, the Welsh Nightingale. It is the stories of the bells that are most enchanting, however.

One story is that Idris Gawr, a giant who used to sit on Cadair Idris (hence its name - Idris' Chair), carried a huge bell. He used to paddle in the river Dyfi but was drowned in a storm and his great bell lost in the sands, still to be heard at times. A more modern tale is that the bells were brought from Flanders to Aberdyfi church tower, but the ship carrying them was threatened in a storm before the heavy bells could be landed, so they were dumped overboard as a safety precaution. This story is hard to swallow as Aberdyfi didn't have its own church until after Dibdin's death in 1814. More likely is the one about bells being tied around the necks of sheep in the ancient past, as with modern Swiss cows. Menna, a shepherdess, sang to their accompaniment as she kept watch for her sailor lover to return.

The favourite story, however, is of Cantre'r Gwaelod (the Lowland Hundred), a once-fertile plain now covered by Cardigan Bay. According to legend, this most fertile part of the Lord of Ceredigion's land was drowned in the 6th century. This undoubtedly happened, although modern geologists date the event as no later than 3500 BC. Remains of tree stumps of submerged forests can still be seen. There are distinctive submerged reefs bordering this area to the south and north to mark its possible boundaries - Sarn y Bwch near Tywyn and Sarn Gynfelyn between Borth and Aberystwyth.

The seaward side of Cantre'r Gwaelod had to be protected by strong walls or dykes. Gwyddno Garanhir, Lord of Ceredigion, entrusted these defences to Seithennin, but this notorious drunkard neglected his duty and a storm broke the walls while he was at a feast. The whole area was inundated and Manua, the chief settlement which contained the bells, drowned. Taliesin the bard escaped, as did Gwyddno, but Seithennin perished and his sons had to atone for his misdeeds, becoming Celtic saints and founding churches.

Aberdyfi's isolated position has encouraged history to pass it by, although it seems always to have been an important crossing point from North to South Wales. In 1216, Llywelyn ap Iorwerth called all Welsh rulers to the Great Council of Aberdyfi, in an attempt to unite Wales. Only three houses were recorded at "Devye" in 1569, but herring fishermen from all parts assembled here in season. Great excitement was caused by the arrival of a Spanish ship in 1597. The Spaniards landed on a foraging expedition and defence forces hurriedly mustered to pick off some sailors with musket shots before the Spaniards sailed away.

The local oak forests, now denuded, provided timber for export, while the fish landed here fed southern Meirionnydd in the famine year of 1649. The 18th century saw the growth of lead, silver, zinc and copper exports. Some of these minerals came from Aberdyfi itself. The Company of Mine Adventurers was recorded as shipping lead and copper from Aberdovey in 1708. In 1823 a copper mine was available for leasing just 500 yards from the Dyfi's bank. By then, however, the mineral industry was in decline. The last record of mining in Aberdyfi was the sale of Corbet Dovey copper mine in 1863. This mine was so close to the shore that its ore was loaded directly onto the boats.

The wool trade replaced minerals for a while, but the industrialisation of this industry in Yorkshire halted this development. Instead, the mid 19th century saw the rapid growth of Aberdyfi as a port. Shipbuilding was a thriving local industry, while many locals went to sea, giving Aberdyfi its strong maritime influence, as recorded by the Rev. D.W. Morgan in his book *Brief Glory*, and by the Maritime Museum on the sea front which is run by the local Outward Bound Centre, started here during the Second World War.

The railway reached the southern side of the Dyfi estuary in 1864, heralding the start of the tourist industry. A ferry from the Ynyslas shore transported passengers to Aberdyfi, as it had for centuries. There were plans to bridge the estuary at this point, but the railway finally reached Aberdyfi from Dyfi Junction in 1867, when it was stipulated that the fare from Aberdyfi to Ynyslas (station now closed, but close to Borth) should reflect the former distance by ferry and not the actual rail mileage. A railway line had reached Aberdyfi from the north in 1863, allowing slate from Abergynolwyn to be exported from Aberdyfi harbour (via Tywyn). A 373ft-long jetty allowed ships to be loaded and unloaded even at low tide, while prospects of Aberdyfi becoming an Irish ferry port were provided by the Aberdyfi and Waterford Steamship Co. Ltd, whose services also imported Irish cattle and potatoes. A lifeboat was stationed here and has made several rescues over the years.

Aberdyfi's maritime tradition and its new intake of tourists were catered for by an annual regatta, the first being held here in August 1880. A golf course opened and local families were known to camp out in July and August to release their properties for tourist income. The village grew to boast 1,358 inhabitants in 310 houses in 1901. The church, which wasn't built until 1842

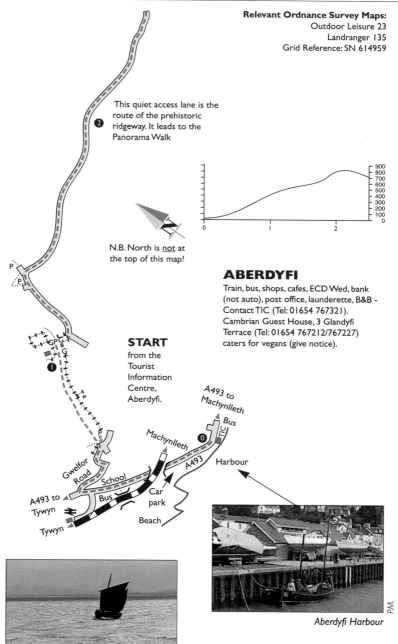

**Relevant Ordnance Survey Maps:**
Outdoor Leisure 23
Landranger 135
Grid Reference: SN 614959

**②** This quiet access lane is the route of the prehistoric ridgeway. It leads to the Panorama Walk

N.B. North is <u>not</u> at the top of this map!

## ABERDYFI

Train, bus, shops, cafes, ECD Wed, bank (not auto), post office, launderette, B&B - Contact TIC (Tel: 01654 767321). Cambrian Guest House, 3 Glandyfi Terrace (Tel: 01654 767212/767227) caters for vegans (give notice).

**START**
from the Tourist Information Centre, Aberdyfi.

A493 to Machynlleth

Bus

TIC ❶

Machynlleth

A493

Harbour

Gwelfor Road

School

Bus

A493 to Tywyn

Car park

Tywyn

Beach

P

P

GPG
S

❶

S

Aberdyfi Harbour

Aberdyfi Bay

P.M.

P.M.

3

(until then worshippers had to travel to Tywyn), finally had its bells installed in 1937. Tourism now reigned supreme, with there being no place for a small port in the  fiercely competitive 20th century. The Outward Bound Centre is a reminder of the past, however, while a ferry may take tourists across to Ynyslas during the season. The Snowdonia  National Park maintains a Tourist Information Centre, and the Seafront Garden Project earned Aberdyfi the Prince of Wales Award for Environmental Improvement in 1972.

At Carn March Arthur we find reminders of King Arthur for the first (but not the last) time on this walk. Carn March Arthur is a rock indented with what is said to be the hoofprint of Arthur's horse. Some say the horse carried Arthur to safety from here to Ynys-hir by leaping across the Dyfi estuary when pursued by his enemies, or that the mark was left after King Arthur's horse had dragged a large, hairy monster out of Llyn Barfog, the nearby lake. Others say it was Huw Gadarn, or Huw the Mighty, who captured a local monster and dragged it into the lake, where it was drowned. This Huw Gadarn is as interesting a character as Arthur, for he is said to have led the first colony of Cymri into Britain from Defrobane, where Istanbul now stands, about 1800 BC. The educational system of the druids is traced to Huw Gadarn, who is said to have mnemonically systematised the wisdom of the ancestors of those people whom he had led west. He was regarded as the personification of intellectual culture and is commemorated for having made poetry the vehicle of memory and to have invented the Triads. To him is attributed the founding of Stonehenge and the introduction of glass-making and writing in Ogham characters. An ox was depicted on his standard, perhaps depicting the sign of Taurus and being the origin of the sobriquet John Bull. He established that a Gorsedd or assembly of druids and bards must be held on an open, uncovered, grass space, in a conspicuous place in full view and hearing of the people. Llyn Barfog means the Bearded Lake. This may refer to the flowery covering on the surface of the lake (water-lilies could be in flower any time from late June to early September), although it is said to commemorate one of King Arthur's knights — "the bearded one". Barfog may even refer to King Arthur's foster father. The lake is most famous for a fairy-tale, however.

The story takes various forms, but the essence is that a fairy-cow from the Llyn Barfog area came into the possession of a poor farmer from Dysyrnant (1/2 mile north of the lake). It bore him fine calves, gave plenty of rich milk and brought luck and wealth. When the cow grew old, however, the farmer decided to slaughter her. When the time came, the knife fell from the hand of the butcher and from the rocks above the lake a little green fairy woman called the cow home. The cow and her calves disappeared into the lake along with the fairy woman and the farmer soon found his luck had deserted him.

Pennal is an ancient site. The Romans built a fort to accommodate a

**Relevant Ordnance Survey Maps:**
Outdoor Leisure 23
Landranger 135

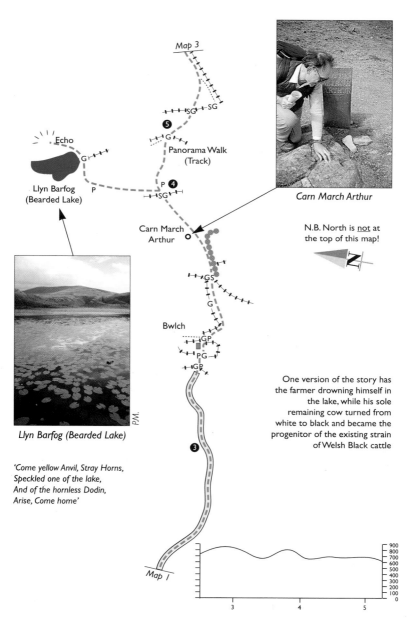

Map 3

Echo

⊕⊕ SG ⊢ SG

**5**

G

Panorama Walk
(Track)

P **4**
SG

Carn March Arthur

Echo

G

Llyn Barfog    P
(Bearded Lake)

*Carn March Arthur*

N.B. North is <u>not</u> at
the top of this map!

Carn March    O
Arthur

GS

G

Bwlch

GP

PG

GP

*Llyn Barfog (Bearded Lake)*

'Come yellow Anvil, Stray Horns,
Speckled one of the lake,
And of the hornless Dodin,
Arise, Come home'

One version of the story has
the farmer drowning himself in
the lake, while his sole
remaining cow turned from
white to black and became the
progenitor of the existing strain
of Welsh Black cattle

**3**

P.M.

Map 1

900
800
700
600
500
400
300
200
100
0

3          4          5

**Relevant Ordnance Survey Maps:**
Outdoor Leisure 23
Landranger 135

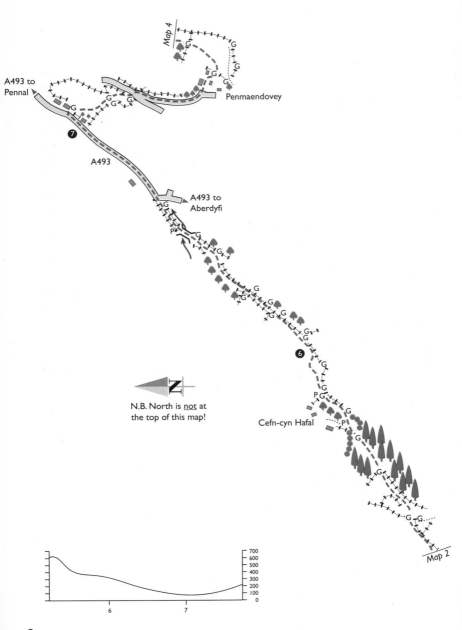

N.B. North is <u>not</u> at
the top of this map!

A493 to
Pennal

Penmaendovey

A493

A493 to
Aberdyfi

Cefn-cyn Hafal

Map 4

Map 2

*The view from Talgarth Woods, facing south.*

garrison of 500 men at Cefn-caer, 600 yards south-east of the present village. This fort was on Sarn Helen, the Roman road from Caerhun, near Conwy, to Maridunum (Carmarthen), and occupied a strategic ridge 50 feet above the river's floodplain, which surrounded it on three sides, and near an ancient ford. It could be conveniently served from the sea by way of the Dyfi estuary. Roman coins, a gold chain, bricks, pottery and tiles have been found here and Roman bricks were visible in the walls of Pennal church before it was demolished in 1769 prior to rebuilding. The circular graveyard indicates an ancient pre-Christian site.

Remains of a Roman hypocaust were also found at Cefn-caer in 1865 but little remains now, just grassy banks with a farmhouse set in what was the west corner of the fort. This may have been Maglona, where a Thracian cavalry unit was stationed.

The Tomen Las or Green Mound between Pennal and Talgarth is probably the site of a medieval Ilys or court. Owain Glyndŵr summoned a parliament here in 1404 which agreed to pledge the Welsh church's allegiance to the French-backed Avignon Pope Benedict XIII. St David's, now an archbishopric, was free of Canterbury's dominance, while universities were planned for both North and South Wales

Pennal's church is one of only four churches in the world dedicated to St Peter ad Vincula (in chains). The others are at the Tower of London, Rome and the Syrian Monastery in Jerusalem where St Peter was freed from his chains.

Pennal church hall houses an interesting exhibition of the village's history. Ask the rector for the key to see it. The rectory is the last house on the left as the A493 leaves Pennal for Machynlleth. The church hall is near the war memorial and plaque to the memory of six crew members of an RAF Wellington bomber, based at Moreton-in-Marsh, Glos, who died when their plane crashed into Ffridd Rhosfarch, the hillside above Pennal, on August 17th, 1941, while on a cross-country training flight in low cloud.

*Tomen Las*
*between Pennal*
*and Talgarth*

**Relevant Ordnance Survey Maps:**
Outdoor Leisure 23
Landranger 135
Grid Reference: SH 699004

# PENNAL

Bus, shop, post office
ECD Wed, B&B
Riverside Hotel
Tel: 01654 791285
(Vegans please give notice)

N.B. North is not at
the top of this map!

A493 to
Machynlleth

School

A493 to
Aberdyfi

Bus

Tomen
Las

Afon
Pennal

Cefn-caer

Afon
Cwrt

N

Ask the farmer's (Mr Rowlands)
permission before visiting the
site of Cefn-caer (Roman fort).

Talgarth

300
200
100
0

8

8

S
S    G

Map 3

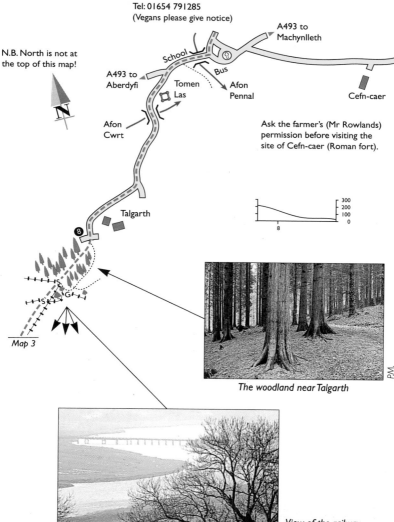

*The woodland near Talgarth*

P.M.

P.M.

*View of the railway
bridge across Afon Dyfi
in the south west*

# Pennal - Corris

## Section Two (miles 8¾ - 19 )

**Relevant Ordnance Survey Maps:**
Outdoor Leisure 23
Pathfinder 885
Landranger 135
Grid Reference: SH 699004

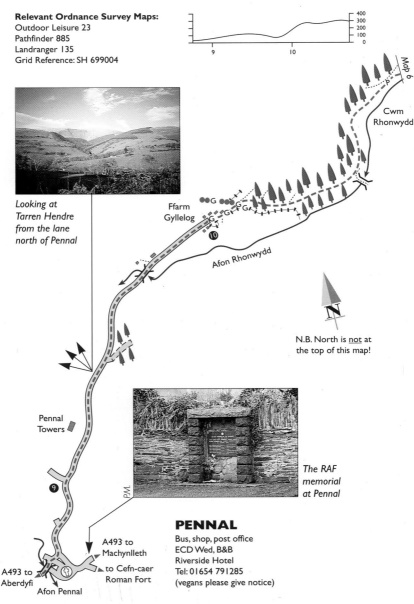

*Looking at Tarren Hendre from the lane north of Pennal*

Cwm Rhonwydd

Map 6

Ffarm Gyllelog

Afon Rhonwydd

N.B. North is not at the top of this map!

Pennal Towers

P.M.

*The RAF memorial at Pennal*

A493 to Machynlleth

to Cefn-caer Roman Fort

A493 to Aberdyfi

Afon Pennal

## PENNAL

Bus, shop, post office
ECD Wed, B&B
Riverside Hotel
Tel: 01654 791285
(vegans please give notice)

10

**Relevant Ordnance Survey Maps:**
Outdoor Leisure 23
Pathfinder 885
Landranger 124 & 135

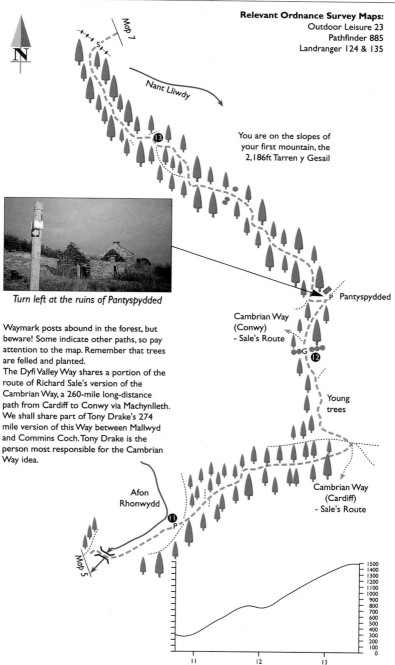

Map 7

Nant Lliwdy

N

You are on the slopes of
your first mountain, the
2,186ft Tarren y Gesail

*Turn left at the ruins of Pantyspydded*

Pantyspydded

Cambrian Way
(Conwy)
- Sale's Route

Young
trees

Waymark posts abound in the forest, but
beware! Some indicate other paths, so pay
attention to the map. Remember that trees
are felled and planted.
The Dyfi Valley Way shares a portion of the
route of Richard Sale's version of the
Cambrian Way, a 260-mile long-distance
path from Cardiff to Conwy via Machynlleth.
We shall share part of Tony Drake's 274
mile version of this Way between Mallwyd
and Commins Coch. Tony Drake is the
person most responsible for the Cambrian
Way idea.

Cambrian Way
(Cardiff)
- Sale's Route

Afon
Rhonwydd

Map 5

**Relevant Ordnance Survey Maps:**
Outdoor Leisure 23
Pathfinder 885
Landranger 124 & 135
Grid Reference: SH 749043

The old Corris Railway ran along
the side of the A487 road nearer
the river (Afon Dulas). Sarn Helen,
the old Roman road, probably
followed the same course

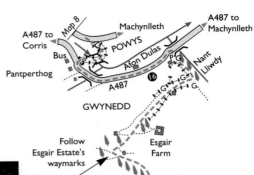

Follow
Esgair Estate's
waymarks

Esgair
Farm

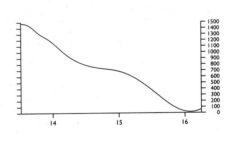

PUBLIC
FOOT PATH
TO
MAIN ROAD

*Follow the signposted path through
Esgair Estate down to the A487*

N.B. North is <u>not</u> at
the top of this map!

Nant
Lliwdy

Old
Level

Old
Level

Map 6

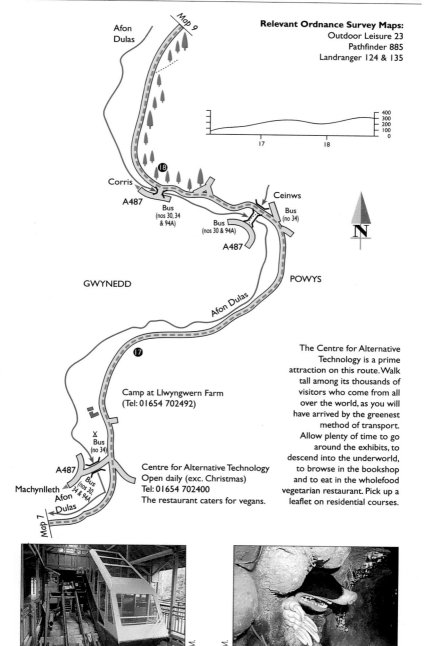

Afon
Dulas

Map 9

**Relevant Ordnance Survey Maps:**
Outdoor Leisure 23
Pathfinder 885
Landranger 124 & 135

Corris

A487

Bus
(nos 30, 34
& 94A)

Bus
(nos 30 & 94A)

Ceinws

Bus
(no 34)

A487

N

GWYNEDD

POWYS

Afon Dulas

Camp at Llwyngwern Farm
(Tel: 01654 702492)

X
Bus
(no 34)

A487

Machynlleth
Afon
Dulas

Bus
(nos 30,
34 & 94A)

Centre for Alternative Technology
Open daily (exc. Christmas)
Tel: 01654 702400
The restaurant caters for vegans.

Map 7

The Centre for Alternative
Technology is a prime
attraction on this route. Walk
tall among its thousands of
visitors who come from all
over the world, as you will
have arrived by the greenest
method of transport.
Allow plenty of time to go
around the exhibits, to
descend into the underworld,
to browse in the bookshop
and to eat in the wholefood
vegetarian restaurant. Pick up a
leaflet on residential courses.

The cliff railway at the Centre for
Alternative Technology (C.A.T.)

Megan the Mole in the C.A.T. Underworld

**13**

Corris is most famous for its slates, indeed its name may even be a Welsh corruption of the English word quarries. The Romans may have quarried for slate here as Sarn Helen (the Roman road) seems to have passed nearby. There is a youth hostel in the old school, much frequented by those intending to walk up Cadair Idris from the Talyllyn side. If you have the time, this would make a worthwhile diversion. You should certainly visit the Corris Railway Museum. A narrow-gauge railway used to carry the slates from here to the main line at Machynlleth. It first opened as a tramway worked by horses in 1859, when it continued past Machynlleth to the old port of Derwenlas. Steam engines were introduced in 1879 and a passenger service started in 1883. The Great Western Railway, which had an interest in the competing Crosville buses, suspended passenger services just a year after taking over the line in 1930. Flood damage to the bridge over the Dyfi brought closure in 1948. The Corris Railway Society was formed in 1967 and enough track had been relaid by 1985 to run trains again on selected summer Saturdays. There are a number of interesting craft workshops in the Corris Craft Centre, the beehive buildings of which lie beside the A487 above the village. Allow time to visit King Arthur's Labyrinth (open daily, 10-5, Easter-Oct, Tel: 01654 761584). This labyrinth of tunnels and caverns deep under the mountains is separated from today's world by a boat ride across the centuries. Relive the ancient tales before walking to the site of King Arthur's last battle, at Camlan, just before the Way enters Dinas Mawddwy.

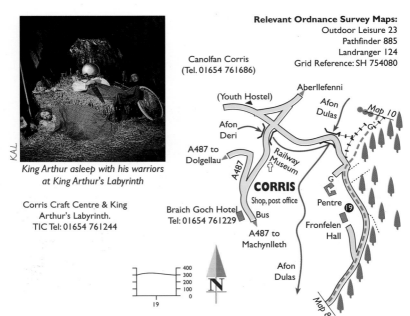

King Arthur asleep with his warriors
at King Arthur's Labyrinth

Corris Craft Centre & King
Arthur's Labyrinth.
TIC Tel: 01654 761244

**Relevant Ordnance Survey Maps:**
Outdoor Leisure 23
Pathfinder 885
Landranger 124
Grid Reference: SH 754080

Canolfan Corris
(Tel. 01654 761686)

Aberllefenni

(Youth Hostel)

Afon
Deri

Afon
Dulas

Map 10

A487 to
Dolgellau

Railway
Museum

**CORRIS**

Shop, post office

Braich Goch Hotel
Tel: 01654 761229

Pentre

19

Bus

Fronfelen
Hall

A487 to
Machynlleth

Afon
Dulas

Map 8

400
300
200
100
0

19

**N**

# Corris - Dinas Mawddwy

## Section Three (miles 19 - 31½)

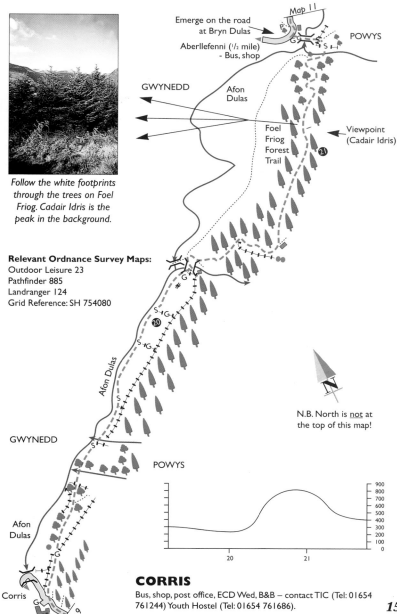

Emerge on the road at Bryn Dulas

Aberllefenni (½ mile) - Bus, shop

Map 11

POWYS

GWYNEDD

Afon Dulas

Foel Friog Forest Trail

Viewpoint (Cadair Idris)

21

*Follow the white footprints through the trees on Foel Friog. Cadair Idris is the peak in the background.*

**Relevant Ordnance Survey Maps:**
Outdoor Leisure 23
Pathfinder 885
Landranger 124
Grid Reference: SH 754080

20

Afon Dulas

GWYNEDD

POWYS

N

N.B. North is not at the top of this map!

Afon Dulas

Corris

Pentre

19

Map 9

900
800
700
600
500
400
300
200
100
0

20          21

## CORRIS

Bus, shop, post office, ECD Wed, B&B – contact TIC (Tel: 01654 761244) Youth Hostel (Tel: 01654 761686).

**15**

**Relevant Ordnance Survey Maps:**
Outdoor Leisure 23
Landranger 124

*Turn right along this waymarked path just before the main forest track bears left.*

The Dyfi Forest is continually changing, with trees being felled and planted.
The Meirionnydd local group of the Ramblers' Association has waymarked the route of the Dyfi Valley Way through it. Take great care to follow the correct path after climbing to a bridleway signpost on your left. Ignoring the track on your left, go ahead with the main track you've been following and, after about 50 yards, pass a rough track on your right. Immediately after this, and opposite a track coming from your left and just before the main track bears left ahead, look for a waymark post on your right bearing a blue arrow on a yellow background. Go right along this path, following the waymarks downhill and through the forest.

N.B. North is <u>not</u> at the top of this map!

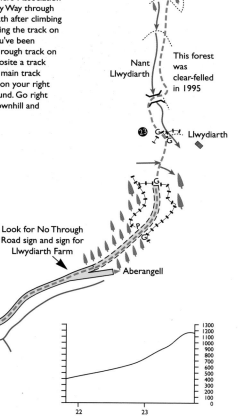

N.B. North is <u>not</u> at
the top of this map!

**Relevant Ordnance Survey Maps:**
Outdoor Leisure 23
Landranger 124

Hendre-ddu Slate & Slab Quarry was established by
Sir Edmond Buckley in the 19th century. He
invested large sums in machinery and quarters for
his men at the quarry. A tramway was built to join
the Mawddwy Railway at Aberangell and an average
of 175 tons of finished slate was being produced
each month by 1876.

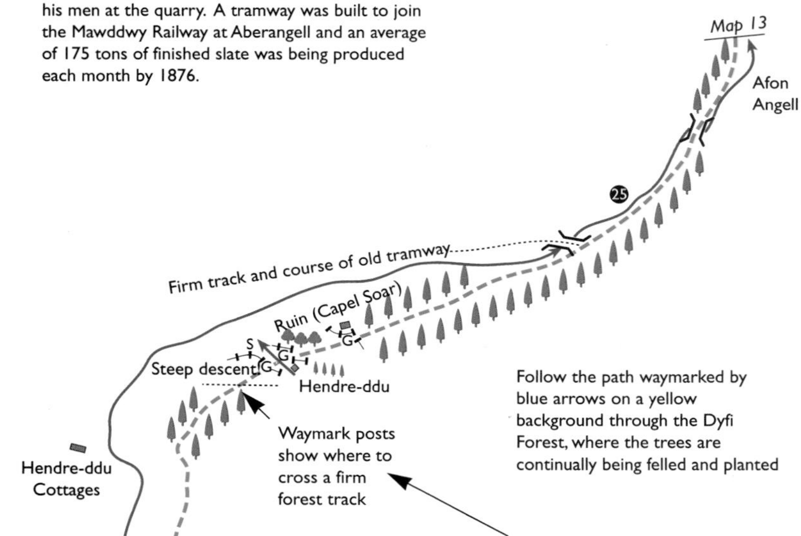

Map 13

Afon
Angell

25

Firm track and course of old tramway

Ruin (Capel Soar)

S
G
Steep descent G

Hendre-ddu

Hendre-ddu
Cottages

Follow the path waymarked by
blue arrows on a yellow
background through the Dyfi
Forest, where the trees are
continually being felled and planted

Waymark posts
show where to
cross a firm
forest track

A waymark post marks
where the path joins
the firm forest track

Hendre-ddu
Quarry (disused)

24

This hillside was
clear of trees in 1995

(Cross a firm
forest track)

Map 11

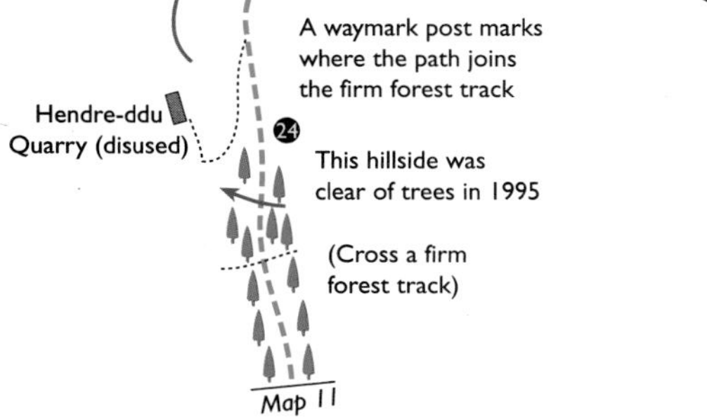

*Waymarking the path
through the Dyfi Forest.*

1200
1100
1000
900
800
700
600
500
400
300
200
100
0

24                    25

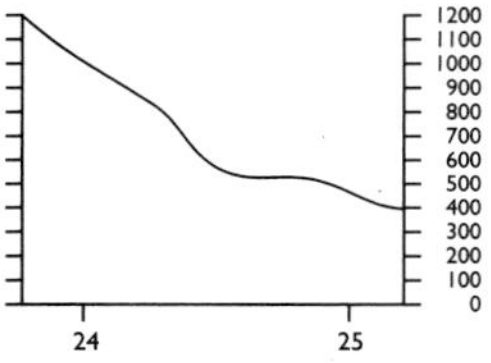

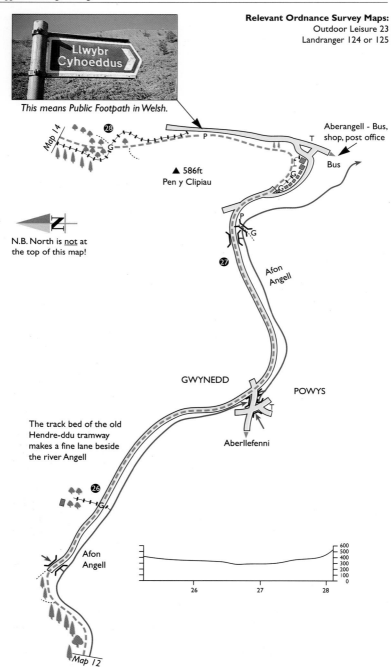

This means Public Footpath in Welsh.

**Relevant Ordnance Survey Maps:**
Outdoor Leisure 23
Landranger 124 or 125

Aberangell - Bus, shop, post office

Bus

Map 14

P

T

▲ 586ft
Pen y Clipiau

N.B. North is not at the top of this map!

P

G

Afon
Angell

GWYNEDD

POWYS

The track bed of the old Hendre-ddu tramway makes a fine lane beside the river Angell

T

Aberllefenni

Afon
Angell

Map 12

600
500
400
300
200
100
0

26      27      28

You are about to walk across the site of King Arthur's last battle, at Camlan. The actual field is Maes-y-Camlan, just before Nant y Gamell (the Crooked Stream, rendered as "Camel" in English), which flows into the nearby Afon Dyfi. The battle probably took place about 570 AD (allowing for the Celtic church's Gnostic practice of dating from the crucifixion and not from Jesus' birth) and was fought between Arthur and his treacherous son and nephew Medrawt (Mordred). Dinas Mawddwy was then part of Maelgwn Gwynedd's territory, and Maelgwn is identified with Sir Lancelot. The local tradition for the battle being here is very strong and is supported by place name and other evidence. The battlefield, Maes-y-Camlan, reaches down to the Dyfi, on the other side of which is Bryn Cleifion, or hillside of the wounded. Above this is Cae'r-gof, some defensive fortifications near the old Roman road which leads towards Nant Saeson, or Saxon stream, where Mordred's Saxon allies camped the night before the battle. Arthur has other connections with this area which we shall come across later — Rhita Gawr and Aran Benllyn, Sir Cai and Caer Gai, while St Tydecho, Mawddwy's patron saint, was Arthur's nephew. The Romans are believed to have mined lead at Blaencywarch, while their road probably crossed the Dyfi where the 17th-century packhorse bridge (Pont Minllyn) still stands. Locals say a castle once stood here, too — could this be the dinas in Dinas Mawddwy? In 1875 during drainage operations behind the Buckley Arms Hotel, an urn was found which contained incinerated bones. Two other urns were said to have been found earlier at the old railway station, now part of Meirion Mill. Local papers of the time tell us that the urn "was found near to the place where it is stated, in some histories, that a castle stood in former years."

*The view looking up the Dyfi Valley from Aberangell.*

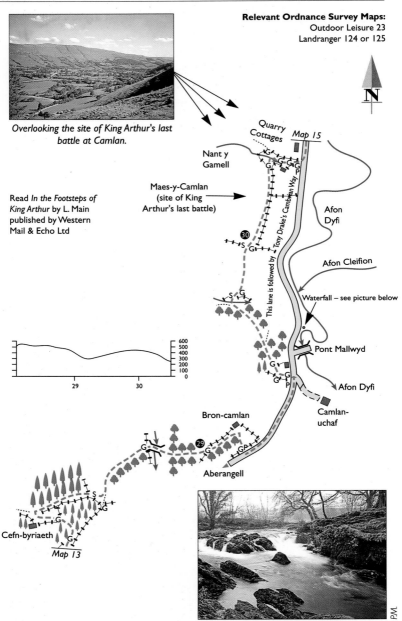

**Relevant Ordnance Survey Maps:**
Outdoor Leisure 23
Landranger 124 or 125

*Overlooking the site of King Arthur's last battle at Camlan.*

Read *In the Footsteps of King Arthur* by L. Main published by Western Mail & Echo Ltd

Quarry Cottages

Map 15

Nant y Gamell

Maes-y-Camlan (site of King Arthur's last battle)

Afon Dyfi

Afon Cleifion

This lane is followed by Tony Drake's Cambrian Way

Waterfall – see picture below

Pont Mallwyd

Afon Dyfi

Camlan-uchaf

Bron-camlan

Aberangell

Cefn-byriaeth

Map 13

*This attractive waterfall was partly created by Sir Edmund Buckley as a salmon leap. The fish were rushed to ice cellars in the old Plas at Dinas Mawddwy.*

P.M.

20

Dinas means a fort or city, while the name Mawddwy may refer to Amwn Ddu, the father of Tydecho, patron saint of Mawddwy. Amwn Ddu married Anna, a daughter of Meurig ab Tewdrig and a sister of King Arthur, making Tydecho Arthur's nephew. It is more likely that the name is even older, however, and refers to Mawdd, a Celtic goddess. Guarded by its mountains, this area has always been a sanctuary and an independent enclave on the fringe of other areas. Mawddwy must have formed part of Maelgwn Gwynedd's territory in the 6th century, as he granted St Tydecho land here as a sanctuary. It was part of Powys in the Middle Ages, however, and did not form part of Merioneth when the county was constituted by the Statute of Rhuddlan in 1284. It wasn't transferred from the Border Marches to Merioneth until the reign of Henry VIII. Remote bureaucrats don't seem to have cut much ice with the people of Mawddwy, however, as what they didn't have officially they assumed unofficially. The very legal existence of the "borough" was doubted in the 19th century, and a Charity Commission enquiry in 1894 concluded that the "borough" had been a mere plaything of the Mytton family, who had come into possession of the lordship of Mawddwy by marriage about the time that it was transferred to Merioneth. Appropriately, the Myttons were descended from Hedd Mdwynog, one of the fifteen tribes of Gwynedd, while Richard Mytton became High Sheriff of Merioneth in 1542. The last of the line was the eccentric Mad Jack Mytton, who was born in 1796. Perhaps the most harmless of his pranks was to offer the local children half a crown to roll down Foel Dinas. At other times he deliberately overturned a gig he was driving so that his nervous friend should have first-hand experience of such a crash. He later rode a bear into his drawing-room in full hunting costume. He died in a debtors' prison at the age of 38.

The lordship of Mawddwy eventually became the property of Sir Edmund Buckley in 1856. About this time, George Borrow passed through, recording in his *Wild Wales* (published 1862) that "Dinas, though at one time a place of considerable importance, if we may judge from its name which signifies a fortified city, is at present little more than a collection of filthy huts. But though a dirty, squalid place, I found it anything but silent and deserted. Fierce looking red-haired men, who seemed as if they might be descendants of the red-haired bandits of old, were staggering about, and sounds of drunken revelry echoed from the huts. I subsequently learned that Dinas was the headquarters of miners, the neighbourhood abounding with mines both of lead and stone". Dinas had indeed been a much more important place, with a population of well over 1000, 12 shops, 14 public houses and several fairs (there were five fairs a year in 1680). Thousands of cattle were sold here, attracting visitors from far afield, some of whom no doubt found themselves in the Great Fetter or Feg Fawr. This was an instrument for punishing

**Relevant Ordnance Survey Maps:**
Outdoor Leisure 23
Landranger 124 or 125

The Red Lion (Gwesty'r Llew Coch) is famous for its traditional Welsh singing on
Saturday nights. Restaurant, B&B, Tel: 01650 531247
B&B and restaurant also at the Buckley Pines Hotel (Tel: 01650 531261) and the
Dolbrodmaeth Inn (Tel: 01650 531333)
Campers are welcome at the Dolbrodmaeth Inn and at Celyn-brithion campsite
(Tel: 01650 531344). Make this your base camp for three nights. Climb the Arans
without a heavy pack, stay in B&B at Llanuwchllyn or Bala (where there is a youth
hostel) and return without a heavy tent to spend the third night in it, already
erected, at Dinas Mawddwy. Meals are served in the Old Station Coffee Shop in
the Meirion Mill.

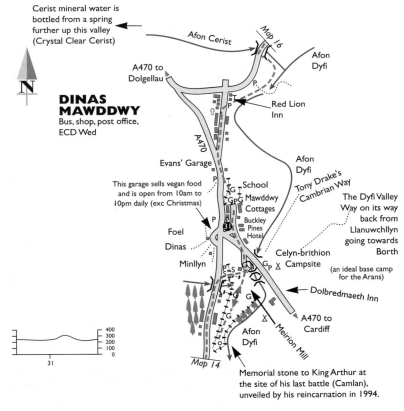

Cerist mineral water is
bottled from a spring
further up this valley
(Crystal Clear Cerist)

**N**

A470 to
Dolgellau

**DINAS
MAWDDWY**
Bus, shop, post office,
ECD Wed

Afon Cerist

Map 16

Afon
Dyfi

Red Lion
Inn

Evans' Garage

A470

This garage sells vegan food
and is open from 10am to
10pm daily (exc Christmas)

Foel
Dinas

Minllyn

Afon
Dyfi

Tony Drake's
Cambrian Way

School

Mawddwy
Cottages

Buckley
Pines
Hotel

The Dyfi Valley
Way on its way
back from
Llanuwchllyn
going towards
Borth

(an ideal base camp
for the Arans)

Celyn-brithion
Campsite

Dolbredmaeth Inn

A470 to
Cardiff

Afon
Dyfi

Meirion Mill

400
300
200
100
0

31

Map 14

Memorial stone to King Arthur at
the site of his last battle (Camlan),
unveiled by his reincarnation in 1994.

N.B. In Winter, the Meirion Mill is closed and there is no access through its gates
onto the A470. If arriving then continue along the lane to reach the A470 at the
garage (and shop) at Minllyn. These gates are also shut on summer evenings so
continue using the lane then, too.

drunkenness peculiar to Dinas Mawddwy and which offenders especially dreaded. Sir Edmund Buckley re-invigorated the place, investing his family's wealth, which had been gained in Manchester. The old manor house was pulled down and a noble mansion, Plas Dinas, built in its place. The Mawddwy Railway connected Dinas with the Cambrian Railway at Cemmaes Road, seven miles away, in 1868. Such was the vision of the Victorian railway pioneers that it was planned to extend the line to join the GWR at Llanuwchllyn, tunnelling under the Arans! Unfortunately, Sir Edmund Buckley overreached himself and had to file a petition at Manchester County Court for liquidation of his affairs in 1876. The family continued to live in Plas Dinas until 1900, but a fire in 1917 burnt the mansion down.

*The Buckley Pines Hotel, Dinas Mawddwy*

# Dinas Mawddwy -
# Llanuwchllyn

## Section Four (miles 31½ - 43)

*The Red Lion Inn, Dinas Mawddwy.*

**Relevant Ordnance Survey Maps:**
Outdoor Leisure 23
Landranger 124 or 125
Grid Reference: SH 859149

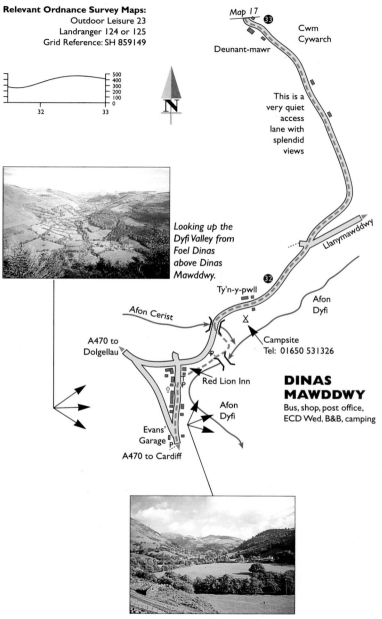

Map 17

Cwm
Cywarch

Deunant-mawr

This is a
very quiet
access
lane with
splendid
views

Llanymawddwy

*Looking up the
Dyfi Valley from
Foel Dinas
above Dinas
Mawddwy.*

Afon Cerist

Ty'n-y-pwll

Afon
Dyfi

A470 to
Dolgellau

Campsite
Tel: 01650 531326

Red Lion Inn

Afon
Dyfi

## DINAS
## MAWDDWY

Bus, shop, post office,
ECD Wed, B&B, camping

Evans'
Garage

A470 to Cardiff

*The view up the Dyfi Valley from
Dinas Mawddwy.*

The head of Cwm Cywarch was an important mining area. The Romans probably mined lead here, while the local squire, Mytton, worked the mine, extracting about 80 tons of ore, before 1770. An energetic woman named Elisabeth Baker, one of several lessees from the Crown of extensive tracts of land, including the Aran mountains, considered it as part of her lease in August 1770, noting that Squire Mytton no doubt abandoned the mine because he would have been stopped by the Lords of the Treasury if he had taken more. This would have exposed him to his tenants as being of only limited power, so he pretended the mine wasn't worth working any more. Mytton objected to Mrs Baker's operations and did all he could to frustrate her. New investment in 1851 failed to pay off, however, and only 349 tons of lead was extracted from 1845 to 1862. The oldest workings can be seen to the west, beyond the Mountain Club hut, Bryn Hafod, which was opened in 1965.

*Looking across the Dyfi Valley from Foel Dinas at the rhododendron on Cefn Coch.*

**Relevant Ordnance Survey Maps:**
Outdoor Leisure 23
Landranger 124 or 125

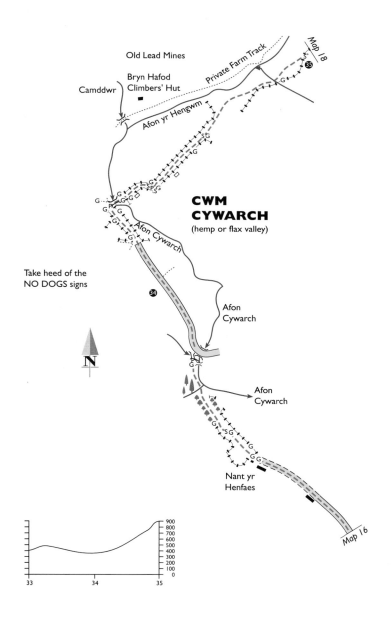

Old Lead Mines

Bryn Hafod
Climbers' Hut

Camddwr

Private Farm Track

Map 18

Afon yr Hengwm

# CWM
# CYWARCH
(hemp or flax valley)

Take heed of the
NO DOGS signs

Afon Cywarch

N

Afon
Cywarch

Afon
Cywarch

Nant yr
Henfaes

Map 16

**Relevant Ordnance Survey Maps:**
Outdoor Leisure 23
Landranger 124 or 125

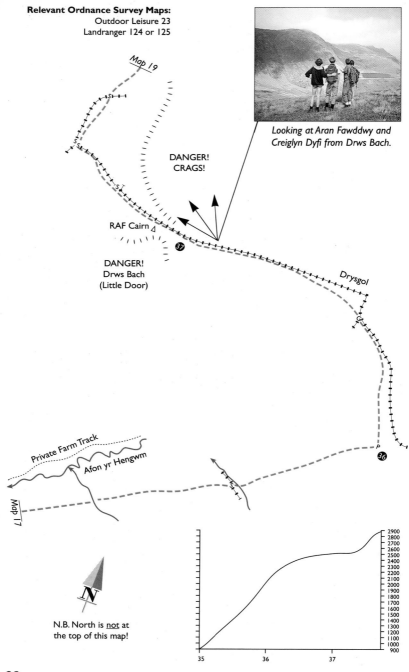

*Looking at Aran Fawddwy and Creiglyn Dyfi from Drws Bach.*

Map 19

DANGER!
CRAGS!

RAF Cairn △

Drysgol

DANGER!
Drws Bach
(Little Door)

Private Farm Track

Afon yr Hengwm

Map 17

N.B. North is *not* at
the top of this map!

Aran Fawddwy is 2971ft high. Although obviously a strenuous climb, it is well worth the effort, and on a fine day it is a real joy. The climb is never difficult (but keep close to the fence at Drws Bach) and is open to all with the stamina. The most important thing is to choose your weather and be prepared for any sudden deterioration. This means carrying spare warm, wind-and-rain-proof clothing, emergency food rations and having the good sense to turn back if necessary. You must also wear good walking boots, carry a map and compass, and have left word of where you are going and when you expect to be back. This route is straightforward, having the aid of convenient fences for navigation.

Aran Fawddwy is regaining its popularity with walkers after access problems in the early 1980s. The establishment of courtesy paths, which are marked on maps displayed at the start of the climb and along the route, have led to stiles for erection over fences being air-lifted to a height of nearly 3000 ft.

There are warning notices about dogs and it is most important that these are heeded. The Animals Act 1971 states that dogs endangering livestock may be shot. The Protection of Livestock Act 1953 makes it an offence to permit a dog to worry livestock, with a maximum penalty of £200. Worrying includes being at large in a field in which there are sheep.

As you reach Drws Bach, the "little door" which gives access to Aran Fawddwy, notice the cairn built by members of RAF St Athan mountain rescue team in memory of SAC Mike Aspain, who on 5th June, 1960, was killed by lightning near this spot whilst on duty with the team. Stop to sign the book in the heavy box at its base. This is also a good place to look right across Craiglyn Dyfi, the lake which is the source of the Afon Dyfi, and to photograph the Aran range.

*On Drysgol, descending from Aran Fawddwy.*

On your left as you climb up to Aran Fawddwy's ridge is the site of a war-time aircrash. A photo-reconaissance Mosquito crashed here whilst on a cross-country exercise on 9th February, 1944. The plane was based at RAF Benson (Oxon) with 540 squadron and had survived 16 sorties over Europe.

The wreckage was finally found on 14th February, 1944, with the dead bodies of both the Polish pilot and the British navigator. A year and a day after this crash, a Bristol Beaufighter crashed below Aran Fawddwy's summit on 10th February, 1945. It was based at Pershore with No 1 Ferry Unit. In snow and ice, both the Australian pilot and the British navigator were killed instantly. In between these crashes, on 16th September, 1944, a Republic P-47 Thunderbolt dived into Aran Fawddwy near its summit, killing the pilot.

There is a huge cairn on Aran Fawddwy's summit, reputedly built by the men of Mawddwy when they heard that Cadair Idris was just a few feet higher than their mountain. They could have saved their energy as Aran Fawddwy is a good 43ft higher than its more famous rival — it is also the highest mountain in Britain south of the Snowdon ridge. Its summit affords some excellent views, with Llyn Tegid (Bala Lake), the largest natural lake in Wales, to the north (just to your left as you look along the ridge from Aran Fawddwy to Aran Benllyn), with Arenig Fawr (2800ft) to its left. Sweeping left (westwards) you may just see the 3560ft summit of Snowdon on the horizon, while the bumps of the Rhinogs (highest point Y Llethr, 2475ft) run like a reptile's spine down to the Mawddach estuary, giving you a glimpse of sand on a clear day if the tide is out. Even further round to the left are Cadair Idris (2928ft) and Pumlumon (2468ft), in the south. On your right are the Berwyns and Offa's Dyke. A splendid place on a fine day!

The Arans were the haunt of the giant Rhita Gawr around 500, in the time of the young future King Arthur, who was brought up nearby at Caer Gai with his foster-brother Sir Cai (grid ref: SH 877314). Rhita had the presumption to demand Arthur's beard to add to his collection. Arthur fought Rhita and killed him, probably burying him at Tan-y-Bwlch (grid ref: SH 912244).

It is a fact that the Mawddwy district has produced several reputed giants, including Llewelyn Fawr of Pen-y-gell, Llanymawddwy, while near Cilwern, Llanymawddwy, bones were discovered which were bigger than a normal man's. If a race of giants had to seek a remote sanctuary, why not this area? There <u>were</u> giants on the earth in those days.....

*Overlooking Creiglyn Dyfi from Aran Fawddwy.*

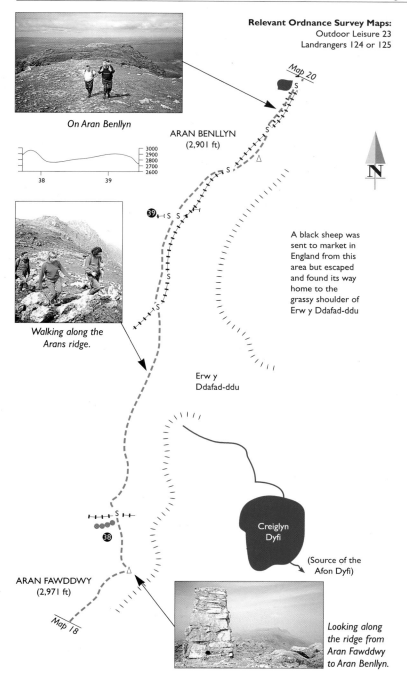

On Aran Benllyn

**Relevant Ordnance Survey Maps:**
Outdoor Leisure 23
Landrangers 124 or 125

Map 20

ARAN BENLLYN
(2,901 ft)

39

Walking along the
Arans ridge.

A black sheep was
sent to market in
England from this
area but escaped
and found its way
home to the
grassy shoulder of
Erw y Ddafad-ddu

Erw y
Ddafad-ddu

Creiglyn
Dyfi

(Source of the
Afon Dyfi)

ARAN FAWDDWY
(2,971 ft)

Map 18

Looking along
the ridge from
Aran Fawddwy
to Aran Benllyn.

**31**

**Relevant Ordnance Survey Maps:**
Outdoor Leisure 23
Landranger 124 or 125

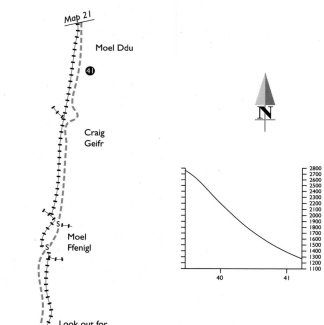

Map 21

Moel Ddu

41

Craig
Geifr

S

S

Moel
Ffenigl

Look out for
Lake Vyrnwy in
the distance on
your right (as
you descend
towards
Llanuwchllyn)

40

Llyn Lliwbran

S

Map 19

*Descending towards Bala Lake from Aran Benllyn.*

Take a break from the walk at Llanuwchllyn to ride the Rheilffordd Llyn Tegid (Bala Lake Railway) along the lakeside to Bala, where there is a campsite near the station, a youth hostel and bed-and-breakfast accommodation, plus all the facilities of a small town, including a Snowdonia National Park Visitor Centre. If you miss the train there is also a bus service, while Llanuwchllyn has its own shop and a nearby campsite. The present 1ft 11¹/₂in narrow-gauge line which covers the 4¹/₂ miles to Bala is laid on the bed of the old standard 4ft 8¹/₂in gauge track, which carried trains from the old Barmouth Junction (now Morfa Mawddach) to Ruabon from 1868 until flooding near Penmaenpool heralded its closure in 1965. The Bala Lake Railway reopened this most scenic section in stages from 1972 to 1976.

Llanuwchllyn station canopy was actually brought here from Aberdyfi when that station was downgraded to a halt, so if you came to Wales by train, now you know where it went! Just over a mile to the north of Llanuwchllyn is Caer Gai, the Roman fort which is where King Arthur spent his youth with his foster-brother, Sir Cai. A nearby farm is intriguingly named Llys Arthur – Arthur's Palace (map reference: SH861286). Spencer referred to Arthur's upbringing here in his *Faery Queen*.

> *His dwelling is low in a valley green,*
> *Under the foot of Rauran mossy hole*
> (Rauran is Aran).

The Llanuwchllyn area has been the home of some great Welsh patriots and advocates of the Welsh language, including Sir Owen Morgan Edwards. His son, Sir Ifan ab Owen Edwards, founded the first all-Welsh school in 1939 and the Urdd Gobaith Cymru (Welsh League of Youth) in 1922.

*The Bala Lake Railway at Llanuwchllyn, with a wave from driver Laurence Main.*

**Relevant Ordnance Survey Maps:**
Outdoor Leisure 18 & 23
Landranger 124 & 125
Grid Reference: SH 880300

# LLANUWCHLLYN
(Bus, train, shop, post office)

Campers who haven't left their
tents at Dinas Mawddwy may
camp at Bryn Gwyn Farm,
Llanuwchllyn (Grid ref: SH 865308,
Tel: 016784 687). There are also
campsites at Bala, a short train or
bus ride away. Bala also has a youth
hostel (Tel: 01678 520215).

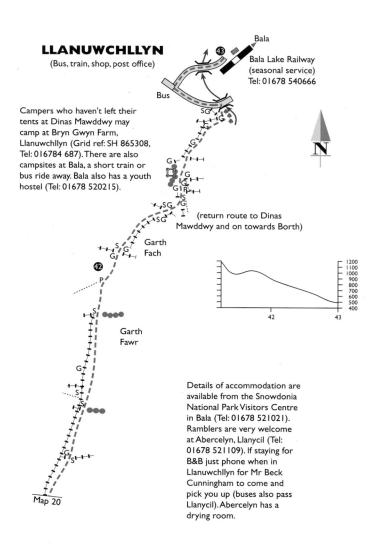

Bala

Bala Lake Railway
(seasonal service)
Tel: 01678 540666

Bus

(return route to Dinas
Mawddwy and on towards Borth)

Garth
Fach

Garth
Fawr

Map 20

Details of accommodation are
available from the Snowdonia
National Park Visitors Centre
in Bala (Tel: 01678 521021).
Ramblers are very welcome
at Abercelyn, Llanycil (Tel:
01678 521109). If staying for
B&B just phone when in
Llanuwchllyn for Mr Beck
Cunningham to come and
pick you up (buses also pass
Llanycil). Abercelyn has a
drying room.

# Llanuwchllyn - Dinas Mawddwy

## Section Five (miles 43 - 61)

*Maid Marian of the Bala Lake Railway, Llanuwchllyn*

**Relevant Ordnance Survey Maps:**
Outdoor Leisures 18 & 23
Landranger 124 or 125
Grid Reference: SH 880300

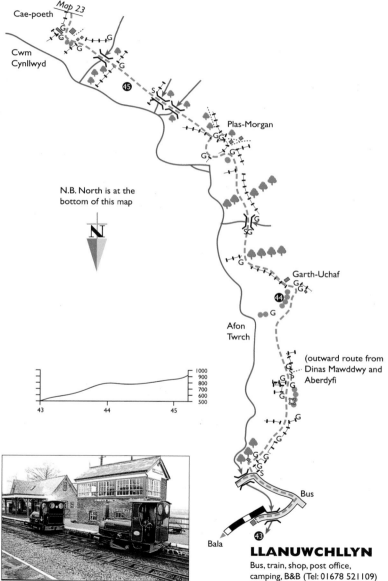

Map 23

Cae-poeth

Cwm
Cynllwyd

45

Plas-Morgan

N.B. North is at the
bottom of this map

**N**

Garth-Uchaf

44

Afon
Twrch

(outward route from
Dinas Mawddwy and
Aberdyfi

1000
900
800
700
600
500

43       44       45

Bus

Bala

43

Bala Lake Railway (seasonal service)
Tel. 01678 540666

# LLANUWCHLLYN

Bus, train, shop, post office,
camping, B&B (Tel: 01678 521109)
(Abercelyn, Llanycil – drying
room & local transport)

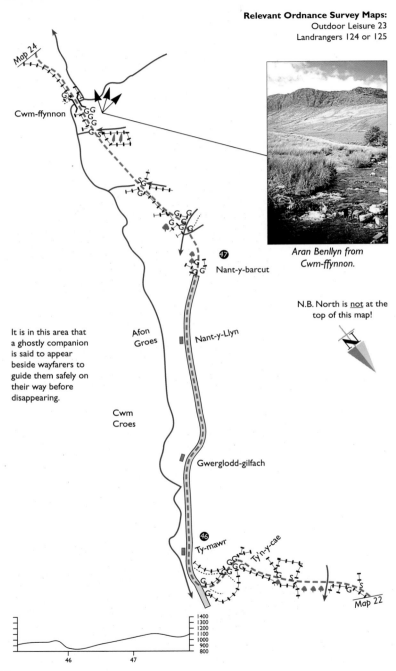

**Relevant Ordnance Survey Maps:**
Outdoor Leisure 23
Landrangers 124 or 125

Map 24

Cwm-ffynnon

**47**

Nant-y-barcut

*Aran Benllyn from
Cwm-ffynnon.*

N.B. North is not at the
top of this map!

Afon
Groes

Nant-y-Llyn

It is in this area that
a ghostly companion
is said to appear
beside wayfarers to
guide them safely on
their way before
disappearing.

Cwm
Croes

Gwerglodd-gilfach

**46**
Ty-mawr

Ty'n-y-cae

Map 22

1400
1300
1200
1100
1000
900
800

46     47

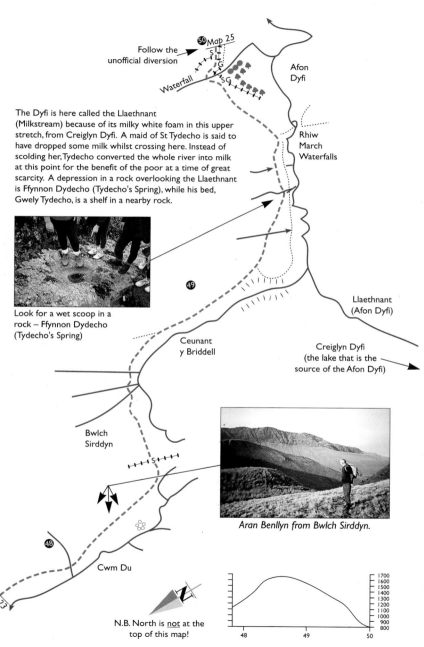

Follow the unofficial diversion

50 Map 25

S
L
G
SG

Waterfall

Afon Dyfi

Rhiw March Waterfalls

The Dyfi is here called the Llaethnant (Milkstream) because of its milky white foam in this upper stretch, from Creiglyn Dyfi. A maid of St Tydecho is said to have dropped some milk whilst crossing here. Instead of scolding her, Tydecho converted the whole river into milk at this point for the benefit of the poor at a time of great scarcity. A depression in a rock overlooking the Llaethnant is Ffynnon Dydecho (Tydecho's Spring), while his bed, Gwely Tydecho, is a shelf in a nearby rock.

Look for a wet scoop in a rock – Ffynnon Dydecho (Tydecho's Spring)

49

Llaethnant (Afon Dyfi)

Ceunant y Briddell

Creiglyn Dyfi (the lake that is the source of the Afon Dyfi)

Bwlch Sirddyn

S

*Aran Benllyn from Bwlch Sirddyn.*

48

Cwm Du

Map 23

N.B. North is not at the top of this map!

1700
1600
1500
1400
1300
1200
1100
1000
900
800

48        49        50

Watch out for a white horse as you approach Bryn Hall. A local lad was once shown a mystery by a ghostly rider here, while visiting motorists have stopped for his white horse, only for it to vanish before their eyes. The ghost seems to be connected with a foul deed at Bryn Hall, where there is a bloodstain on the stairs which defies all attempts to remove it, including changing the wooden boards. It is believed to be the blood of a murdered baby whose mother was a chambermaid but whose father was the estate owner. The ghostly rider is probably the wicked father riding to hide the murdered baby's body in the woods. It is also said that the house can shake violently.

Llanymawddwy is the spiritual centre of Mawddwy and you should make a point of visiting St Tydecho's church. This has long been a holy spot and its Christian nature probably predates St Tydecho, since a tombstone from about 500 AD was found here. Its Latin inscription translates as "(the stone) of the daughter of Salvianus. Here (she) lies, Ve...maie, wife of Tigirnicus, and of his daughter Rigohene. She lies (here), wife of Oneratus..."

The burial of Salvianus himself is recorded at Caer Gai, near Llanuwchllyn, where another stone from about 500AD was dug up with this inscription (in Latin): "Here lies Salvianus Bursocavi(s), son of Cupetianus." Could he be related to Sir Cai, Arthur's foster-brother?

Arthur's nephew, Tydecho, is the saint whose church stands at Llanymawddwy today. Tydecho was the brother of St Samson and a first cousin to St Cadfan. One of three leaders of saints who came back from Brittany to Wales, Tydecho was renowned for his austerity, wearing a hair coat and sleeping on rock.

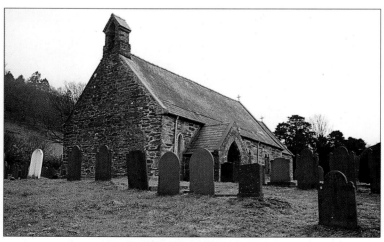

*St Tydecho's Church, Llanymawddy*

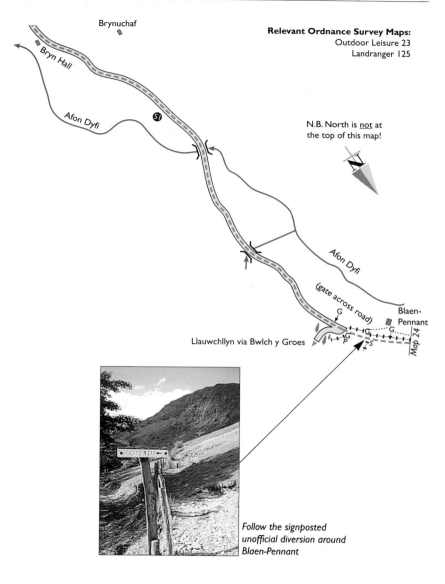

Brynuchaf

Bryn Hall

Afon Dyfi

**57**

**Relevant Ordnance Survey Maps:**
Outdoor Leisure 23
Landranger 125

N.B. North is <u>not</u> at
the top of this map!

**N**

Afon Dyfi

(gate across road)

Blaen-
Pennant

G

G    G    G

Map 24

Llauwchllyn via Bwlch y Groes

G
P    S

*Follow the signposted
unofficial diversion around
Blaen-Pennant*

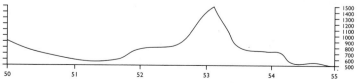

|   | 1500 |
|---|------|
|   | 1400 |
|   | 1300 |
|   | 1200 |
|   | 1100 |
|   | 1000 |
|   | 900 |
|   | 800 |
|   | 700 |
|   | 600 |
|   | 500 |

50        51        52        53        54        55

**41**

# Dyfi Valley Way

**Relevant Ordnance Survey Maps:**
Outdoor Leisure 23
Landranger 125
*N.B. The gradient profile for this map is on page 41.*

The old level in the river bank was probably driven in 1847 and revealed some very pure iron, plus some lead and copper. By 1850 however, it was found not to be commercially viable. This is not to be confused with the Red Dragon gold mine, which has been rediscovered west of Dinas Mawddwy.

Look for a channel which provided water to power the wood saw at Ty-Isaf, near the old Sun Inn, Llanymawddwy

Look for a channel which provided water to power the old waterwheel for churning milk at Brynuchaf

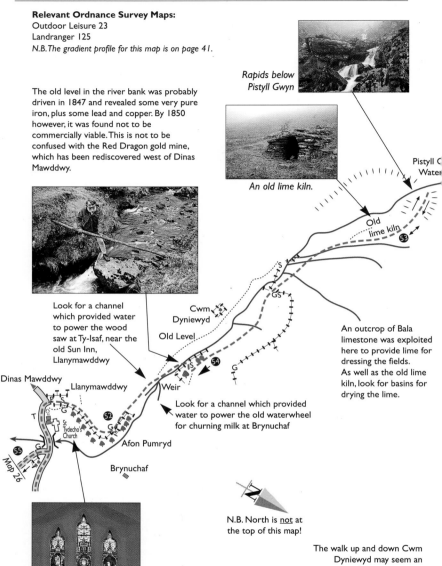

*Rapids below Pistyll Gwyn*

*An old lime kiln.*

Pistyll C
Water

Old lime kiln
53

Cwm Dyniewyd
Old Level

S
GS
iS
54
G

An outcrop of Bala limestone was exploited here to provide lime for dressing the fields. As well as the old lime kiln, look for basins for drying the lime.

Dinas Mawddwy
Llanymawddwy
St Tydecho's Church
T
52
G
Weir
Afon Pumryd
Brynuchaf
Map 26
55

*N.B. North is not at the top of this map!*

*St Tydecho can be seen in the right hand window of the church in Llanymawddwy.*

P.M.

The walk up and down Cwm Dyniewyd may seem an unnecessary diversion on your way between Llanuwchllyn and Dinas Mawddwy, but the beauty and solitude of this valley, crowned by its waterfall, are the essence of the upper reaches of the Afon Dyfi. Read the legend of St Tydecho on the wall at the back of his church in Llanymawddwy.

42

*Looking down Cwm Dyniewyd from above Pistyll Gwyn.*

That great tormentor of saints, Maelgwn Gwynedd, thought one day he would annoy the saint by sending a stud of white horses to be pastured by his prayers.

Tydecho turned them loose on the mountainside and they were found to be fat, despite the conditions. Maelgwn, provoked by this, seized the saint's oxen while at team. The next day, however, wild deer, in place of the oxen, were seen ploughing the land (Dol-y-Ceirw, near the Dyfi) with a grey wolf harrowing after them, so Maelgwn sent a pack of hounds to chase them away and sat down on the blue stone of Tydecho to watch the sport. When he attempted to rise, he found himself stuck to the rock and had to humbly beg the saint's pardon to be freed. On being released, he returned Tydecho's oxen and atoned by giving him the privilege of sanctuary for "a hundred ages," asylum for man and beast and exemption from all fighting, burning and killing.

Pistyll Gwyn, the aptly named "white spout" waterfall, is the reason for this route's diversion up and down Cwm Dyniewyd.

The water drops at least 100 feet down the bare rock face and an interesting side view is possible. Near the base of the waterfall are the remains of an old lime kiln and settling beds, while further down the valley is evidence of mid-19th century mining and more recent early-20th century use of water-power.

The high ground above the sheer dead-end of Cwm Dyniewyd was the scene of a fatal aircrash. At 1.12pm on April 6th, 1942, a Mark IC Vickers Wellington bomber (serial number P9299) belonging to 1429 Flight, took off from its base at East Wretham on a cross-country training flight. The all-Czech pupil crew flew into low cloud, causing them to fly up this valley to their tragic end. All six crew members were killed in the crash.

**Relevant Ordnance Survey Maps:**
Outdoor Leisure 23
Landranger 125

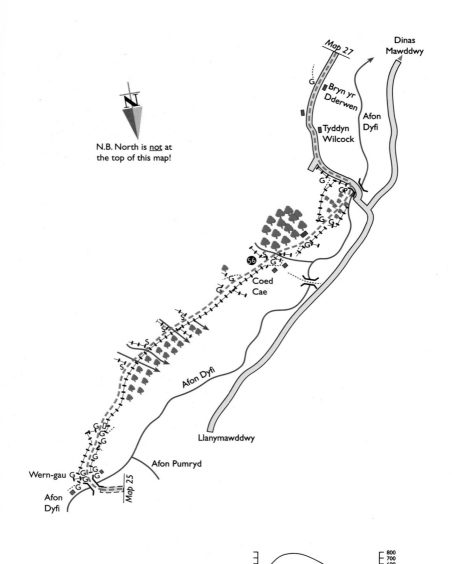

N.B. North is <u>not</u> at
the top of this map!

**Relevant Ordnance Survey Maps:**
Outdoor Leisure 23
Landrangers 124 or 125

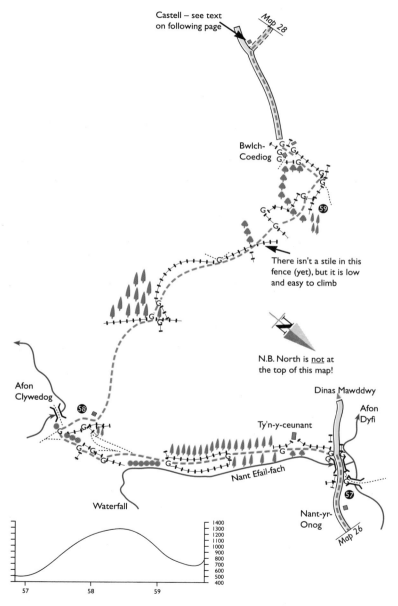

Castell – see text
on following page

Map 28

Bwlch-
Coediog

59

There isn't a stile in this
fence (yet), but it is low
and easy to climb

N.B. North is <u>not</u> at
the top of this map!

Afon
Clywedog

58

Dinas Mawddwy

Afon
Dyfi

Ty'n-y-ceunant

Nant Efail-fach

Waterfall

Nant-yr-
Onog

57

Map 26

45

Castell is an interesting name for a farmhouse. The place is famous for its ghost rather than for a castle, however. It is said that a woman owned this property whose husband visited a mistress elsewhere. When the wife died the husband used the dead woman's hand to forge her will. Later, when her husband was entertaining in the house, a maid went to a locked cabinet to take out her former mistress's favourite crockery. She recoiled in horror when a ghostly hand appeared to stop her unlocking the cabinet door. Other evidence of ghostly activity were cows refusing to enter a cowshed, an apparition of a white cat, furniture shaking and strange sounds in a particular bedroom.

Eventually the family decided to leave for another farmhouse. They had loaded the wagon with furniture but the horses wouldn't pull it. It wasn't until their dead mistress's favourite teapot was taken from the load that the wagon moved. For a long time it was considered necessary to take back anything that was borrowed from the house on the same day that it was borrowed.

Dinas Mawddwy's facilities include bus services, hotels and B&Bs, shops and a post office, ECD Wed.

Dolbrodmaeth Inn
Tel: 01650 531333

Celyn-brithion Campsite
Tel: 01650 531344

Buckley Pines Hotel
Tel: 01650 531261 &

The Red Lion
Tel: 01650 531247.

**Relevant Ordnance Survey Maps:**
Outdoor Leisure 23
Landrangers 124 or 125
Grid Reference: SH 861137

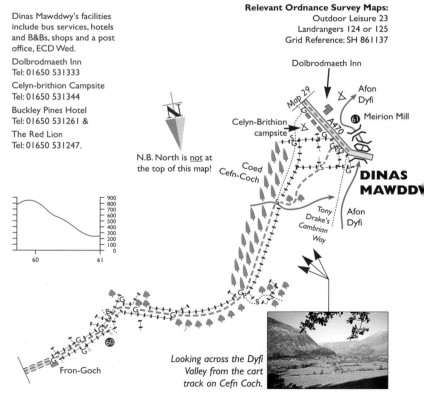

N.B. North is not at the top of this map!

*Looking across the Dyfi Valley from the cart track on Cefn Coch.*

Back in Dinas Mawddwy, our route this time gives a close-up view of the 17th century packhorse bridge Pont Minllyn. It stands between the old railway station, now a coffee shop, and Celyn-Brithion campsite. The Mawddwy railway had a troubled history from 1867, when a government inspector refused it a certificate. Passenger services were temporarily closed in 1901 because of lack of repair of equipment, followed by complete closure in 1908. Absorption into the Cambrian Railway brought a grand re-opening in 1911, soon to be justified by the war traffic to the ammunition which was then stored in Minllyn slate quarry. The end of hostilities did not bring a resumption in the slate industry, however, while buses were to provide competition for the passenger traffic from 1924. As a result, passenger services finished in 1930, although the combined Dovey Valley Sunday Schools' excursion to Aberystwyth ran annually in June until 1939. The Second World War kept the line open for goods, with the quarry warehouse used to store machinery for the Rover car company. As with the Corris Railway, damage to a bridge over the Dyfi led to the line's closure in 1951. The line never paid a single dividend to its shareholders in the 83 years of its existence (the last freight train actually ran on 5th September, 1950) and the track had been lifted by a contractor from Sheffield by May 1952. The station trackbed can be seen near Pont Mallwyd. It is unfortunate that the Mawddwy Railway disappeared just a few years before the era of the "Great Little Trains" for tourists to Wales.

*Pont Minllyn*

# Dinas Mawddwy - Darowen
## Section Six (miles 61 - 77)

George Borrow found Mallwyd a small but pretty village, noting that Dr John Davies was a former rector of its ancient church.

One of the greatest of Welsh scholars, he published a Welsh Grammar in 1621 and a Welsh-Latin Dictionary in 1632, while reputedly checking Bishop Parry's translation of the Bible into Welsh. Dr Davies's wife was a granddaughter (on her mother's side) of Baron Lewis Owen, who was murdered by the Red Bandits of Mawddwy, from whom Mallwyd's Brigands Inn is named. Mallwyd is probably derived from Maen Llwyd, or standing stone — presumably where the church now stands. The church was sited here, and not on higher ground, through supernatural intervention. Tydecho found the building blocks of his church kept removing themselves during the night from the upper hillside to this traditional sacred site down in the valley. Its porch, dated 1641, is adorned with old bones, probably of a prehistoric mammoth, dug up here.

*The bones in Mallwyd Church porch.*

48

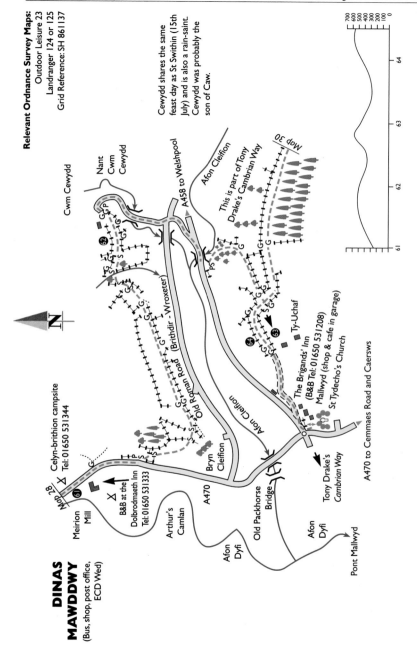

**Relevant Ordnance Survey Maps:**
Outdoor Leisure 23
Landranger 124 or 125
Grid Reference: SH 861137

Cewydd shares the same feast day as St Swithin (15th July) and is also a rain-saint. Cewydd was probably the son of Caw.

Cwm Cewydd

Nant Cwm Cewydd

A458 to Welshpool

Afon Cleifion

This is part of Tony Drake's Cambrian Way

Map 30

Old Roman Road (Brithdir - Wroxeter)

Afon Cleifion

The Brigands' Inn (B&B Tel: 01650 531208)

Ty-Uchaf

Mallwyd (shop & cafe in garage)

St Tydecho's Church

A470 to Cemmaes Road and Caersws

Celyn-brithion campsite
Tel: 01650 531344

Meirion Mill

B&B at the Dolbrodmaeth Inn
Tel: 01650 531333

Map 28

**DINAS MAWDDWY**
(Bus, shop, post office, ECD Wed)

Arthur's Camlan

Bryn Cleifion

A470

Old Packhorse Bridge

Tony Drake's Cambrian Way

Afon Dyfi

Afon Dyfi

Pont Mallwyd

It is worthwhile making the short detour from this route to the burial mound, obscured by trees, near Collfryn. This is where the Red Bandits of Mawddwy (Gwylliaid Cochion Mawddwy) were buried in 1555, some 441 years after their formation in 1114. Their first leader was Owain, son of Cadwgan, son of Bleddyn, who incurred the wrath of Henry I of England in 1107 when he kidnapped Nest, the beautiful daughter of Rhys ap Tewdwr and wife of Gerald of Windsor, custodian of Pembroke Castle. Owain was a prince of Powys and Nest was King Henry's former concubine and the mother of his illegitimate son, the Duke of Gloucester, whose legitimacy would have avoided the war of succession between Stephen and Matilda.

Nest was famed for her beauty and her easily transferable affections. Her abduction by Owain was intolerable to the English, however, who used the excuse to threaten war, and to the Welsh, who saw the affair endangering their fragile independence. Owain took Nest to Plas Eglwyseg, near Llangollen, but it appears that Nest spent some time in Dinas Mawddwy, which was then in Powys. A shop in the village is still called Nant Nest Stores, as it is sited where Nest's house stood — the view from its garden can explain why Nest is said to have loved this spot best of all. Owain was forced to flee to Ireland, however, leaving Nest to make her way back to Pembroke. He returned in 1114 with a band of outlaws from Ireland. Owain died in the fight that ensued after their landing in Pembrokeshire but his outlaws ended up here. "Gwylliaid" is derived from "gwyll" (dusk), when they started on their thefts. They were given the epithet "cochion" either because they had ruddy skin or red hair (or both) or because their hands were red with blood. Mawddwy was virtually an independent outlaw state for over 400 years. The bandits were experts with bows and arrows and were famed for travelling for great distances along the branches of trees without touching the ground. They were finally dealt with by the strong new authority of the Tudors.

Baron Lewis Owen, of Plas Court, Dolgellau, and John Wynn, son of Meredydd of Gwydir, were authorised to punish the clan for their crimes. They came to the bandits' stronghold at Dugoed on Christmas Eve 1554, and captured over 80 of them. Among them was Jac Goch, whose mother pleaded that he be pardoned. When Baron Lewis Owen refused, she bared her breasts and said, "These yellow breasts have given suck to those who shall wash their hands in your blood." Enough bandits remained to carry out this vow of revenge. When the baron next passed this way he was ambushed at a place called Llidiart y Barwn.

**Relevant Ordnance Survey Maps:**
Outdoor Leisure 23
Landranger 124 or 125

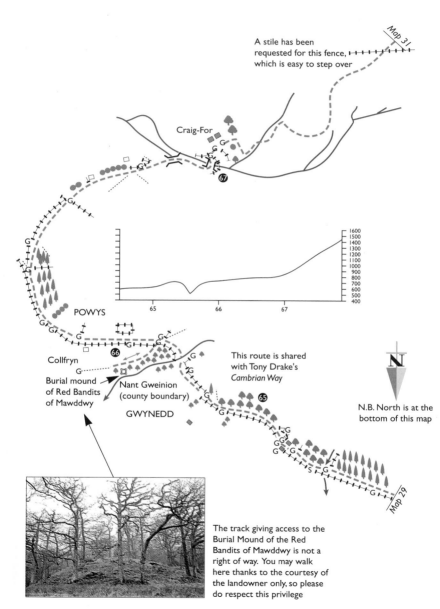

A stile has been
requested for this fence,
which is easy to step over

Map 31

Craig-For

67

POWYS

66

Collfryn

Burial mound
of Red Bandits
of Mawddwy

Nant Gweinion
(county boundary)

GWYNEDD

This route is shared
with Tony Drake's
*Cambrian Way*

65

Map 29

N

N.B. North is at the
bottom of this map

The track giving access to the
Burial Mound of the Red
Bandits of Mawddwy is not a
right of way. You may walk
here thanks to the courtesy of
the landowner only, so please
do respect this privilege

**Relevant Ordnance Survey Maps:**
Outdoor Leisure 23
Pathfinder 886
Landranger 124 or 125

The *Dyfi Valley Way* shares this upland path from Mallwyd to Commins Coch with Tony Drake's *Cambrian Way*, a 274-mile route from Cardiff to Conwy. On a clear day the view is magnificent. The Dyfi is down in the valley on your right (in the west as you walk south).

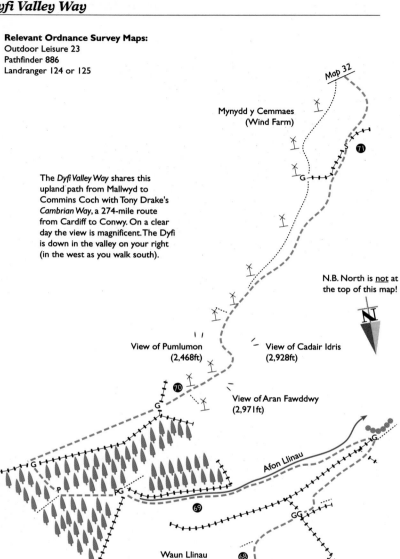

Map 32

Mynydd y Cemmaes
(Wind Farm)

N.B. North is not at the top of this map!

N

View of Pumlumon
(2,468ft)

View of Cadair Idris
(2,928ft)

View of Aran Fawddwy
(2,971ft)

Afon Llinau

Waun Llinau

Map 30

*One of the windmills on Mynydd y Cemmaes.*

*Looking across the Dyfi Valley towards Cadair Idris.*

**Relevant Ordnance Survey Maps:**
Pathfinder 886
Landranger 124 or 125

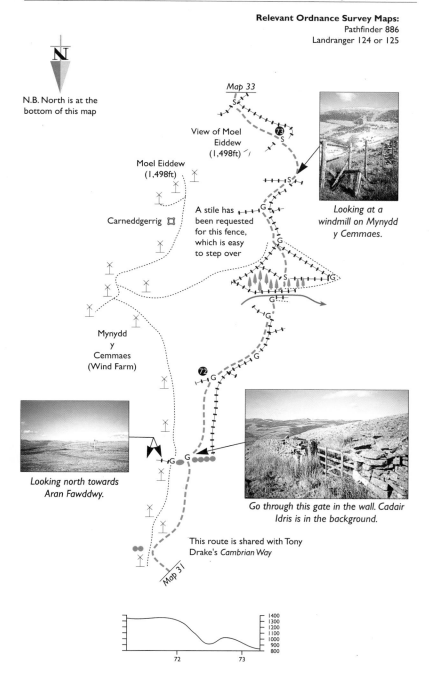

N

N.B. North is at the
bottom of this map

*Map 33*

S

73

View of Moel
Eiddew
(1,498ft)

Moel Eiddew
(1,498ft)

S

Carneddgerrig

A stile has
been requested
for this fence,
which is easy
to step over

G

G

S

G

G

*Looking at a
windmill on Mynydd
y Cemmaes.*

G

G

Mynydd
y
Cemmaes
(Wind Farm)

72 G

G

*Looking north towards
Aran Fawddwy.*

G G

*Go through this gate in the wall. Cadair
Idris is in the background.*

This route is shared with Tony
Drake's *Cambrian Way*

*Map 31*

1400
1300
1200
1100
1000
900
800

72          73

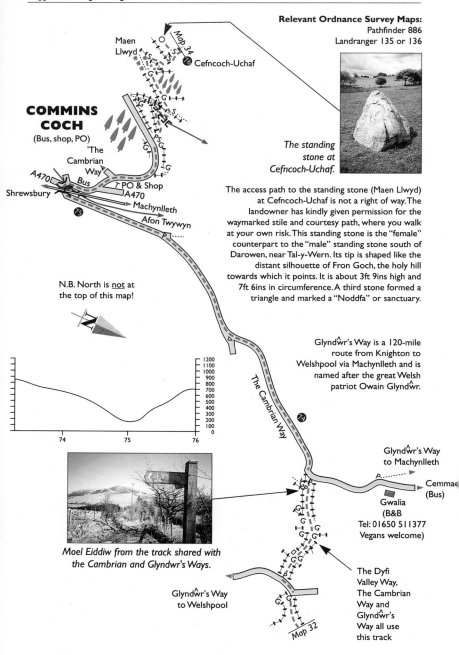

**Relevant Ordnance Survey Maps:**
Pathfinder 886
Landranger 135 or 136

Maen Llwyd

Map 34

Cefncoch-Uchaf

**COMMINS COCH**
(Bus, shop, PO)

'The Cambrian Way'

A470
Shrewsbury
Bus
PO & Shop
A470
Machynlleth
Afon Twywyn

*The standing stone at Cefncoch-Uchaf.*

N.B. North is <u>not</u> at the top of this map!

The access path to the standing stone (Maen Llwyd) at Cefncoch-Uchaf is not a right of way. The landowner has kindly given permission for the waymarked stile and courtesy path, where you walk at your own risk. This standing stone is the "female" counterpart to the "male" standing stone south of Darowen, near Tal-y-Wern. Its tip is shaped like the distant silhouette of Fron Goch, the holy hill towards which it points. It is about 3ft 9ins high and 7ft 6ins in circumference. A third stone formed a triangle and marked a "Noddfa" or sanctuary.

Glyndŵr's Way is a 120-mile route from Knighton to Welshpool via Machynlleth and is named after the great Welsh patriot Owain Glyndŵr.

1200
1100
1000
900
800
700
600
500
400
300
200
100
0

74       75       76

The Cambrian Way

Glyndŵr's Way to Machynlleth

Cemmae (Bus)

Gwalia
(B&B
Tel: 01650 511377
Vegans welcome)

*Moel Eiddiw from the track shared with the Cambrian and Glyndŵr's Ways.*

The Dyfi Valley Way, The Cambrian Way and Glyndŵr's Way all use this track

Glyndŵr's Way to Welshpool

Map 32

The name Darowen is assumed to mean Owen's Oak. The circular graveyard around St Tudyr's Church suggests an ancient site, although the present building was completed in 1864. St Tudyr is buried here and on his festival, October 15th, a young man used to be carried around the parish on his companions' shoulders while others beat him with sticks, perhaps in memory of some persecution endured by the saint.

**Relevant Ordnance Survey Maps:**
Pathfinder 886
Landranger 135 or 136
Grid Reference: SH 830018

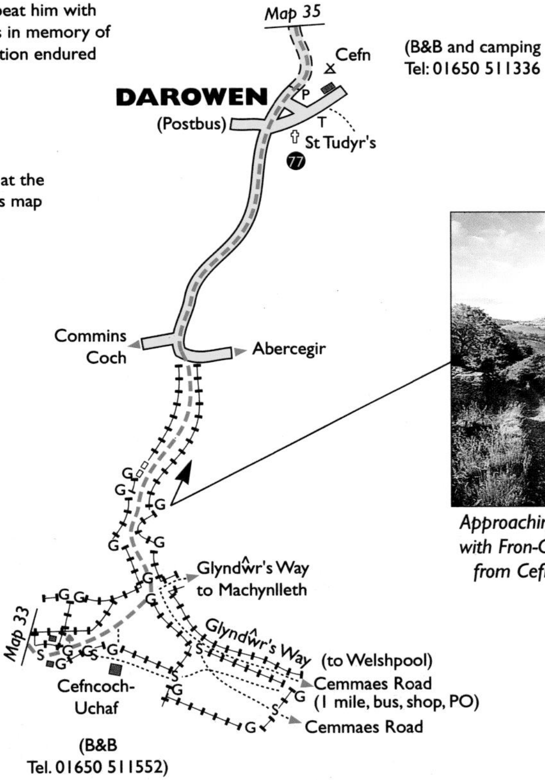

N.B. North is at the bottom of this map

Map 35

Cefn ✕

(B&B and camping Tel: 01650 511336)

**DAROWEN**
(Postbus)

P

St Tudyr's
T

77

N

Commins Coch          Abercegir

*Approaching Darowen, with Fron-Goch in view, from Cefncoch Isaf.*

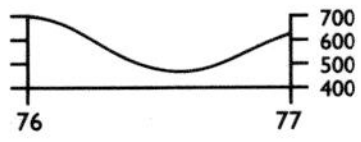

Glyndŵr's Way to Machynlleth

Glyndŵr's Way (to Welshpool)

Map 33

Cefncoch-Uchaf

Cemmaes Road (1 mile, bus, shop, PO)

Cemmaes Road

(B&B Tel. 01650 511552)

700
600
500
400

76          77

The access track to Cefncoch-Uchaf from Glyndŵr's Way isn't a right of way yet. However, the landowner prefers you to take it and hopes the right of way going past his new house will be diverted onto it.

# Darowen - Machynlleth

## Section Seven (miles 77 - 87)

The standing stone near Tal-y-wern is over 6ft high and 12ft 6ins in circumference, and stands in the centre of Cae yr Hen Eglwys (Old Church Field). The remains of an old church were found in this field near the stone, thus reinforcing the view that it was an ancient holy site taken over by the early Christians. This appears to be the "male" stone to the smaller "female" stone at Cefncoch-Uchaf. A third stone once stood to the east of Darowen and was called Carreg y Noddfa. The *Archaeologia Cambrensis* of 1856 refers to "the township of Noddfa, the name of which implies a place of refuge, or a sanctuary, its limits being properly described by three stones."

There is a local tradition of the stones giving sanctuary. Suspected wrongdoers would be given a head start in a race to the stone and would go free if they won. The easy transition to a Christian site may indicate how the druids embraced the new religion early in the Christian era (cf *Celt, Druid and Culde*e by Elder and *The Drama of the Lost Disciples* by Jowett). It is possible, too, that these stones mark leys or earth energy lines.

The road going east from Tal-y-wern is an old drove road, reminding us of the days when the Welsh economy depended on driving herds of cattle to market in England.

*Maen Llwyd standing stone, Tal-y-Wern.*

58

**Relevant Ordnance Survey Maps:**
Pathfinder 886 & 907
Landranger 135 or 136
Grid Reference: SH 830018

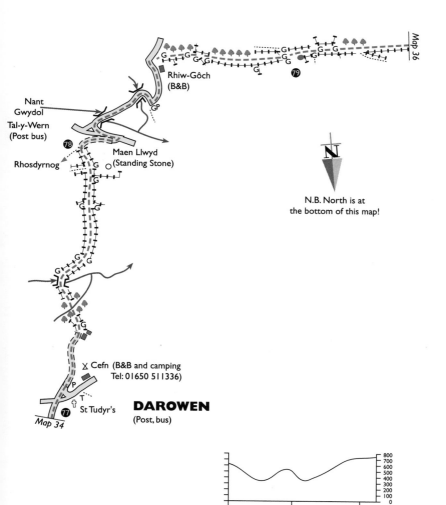

N.B. North is at
the bottom of this map!

**Relevant Ordnance Survey Maps:**
Pathfinder 885, 886 & 907
Landranger 135

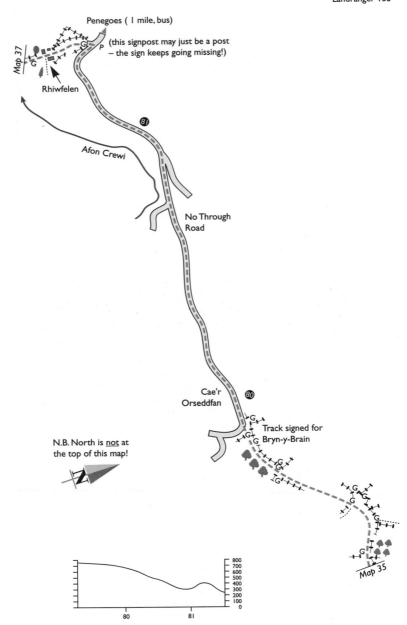

Penegoes ( 1 mile, bus)

(this signpost may just be a post
— the sign keeps going missing!)

Map 37

Rhiwfelen

Afon Crewi

81

No Through
Road

Cae'r
Orseddfan

80

Track signed for
Bryn-y-Brain

N.B. North is *not* at
the top of this map!

Map 35

*Felin Crewi watermill – see page 62.*

The award-winning restored working watermill of Felin Crewi is another of the highlights of this walk. Plan to reach here at a mealtime so that you can enjoy food, made with Felin Crewi's own stoneground flour, in the adjoining café. The old mill was lovingly restored by Mr and Mrs Partridge in the mid-1980s after being disused since the 1940s, when cheaper flour from centralised and faster roller mills made water milling uneconomical. With the demand for more flavoursome and nutritious wholemeal flour increasing, however, a few such mills have made successful comebacks. Oats and wheat are ground, while barley would have been popular when the local farmers depended on this mill for their animal feed. The corn mill has been sited on the banks of the river Crewi since the 18th century, although the original water-wheel would have been smaller than its replacement. A wooden mill race fed the mill pond with water from the weir. A fulling mill or pandy was situated here before the corn mill, as indicated by the name of the cottage on the corner of the approach road. Fulling meant thickening the woollen cloth to make it weatherproof. Until the 1300s this was achieved by treading on it in urine to shrink it.

Later this work was done with wooden mallets driven by a water-wheel. Visitors are welcome to inspect the restoration, while a bird hide is just one outside attraction. Felin Crewi is open every day from Easter to the end of September from 10.30am to 6.00pm, while you can see just the mill working from Mondays to Fridays during the winter. The licensed evening restaurant is open on Fridays and Saturdays from July to September, and Sunday lunches are available between mid-day and 2.00pm. Telephone 01654 703113

Penegoes is said to mean "Head of Egoes", after the legendary Celtic chieftain whose head is reputedly buried beneath a grove of oak trees

*Felin Crewi watermill.*

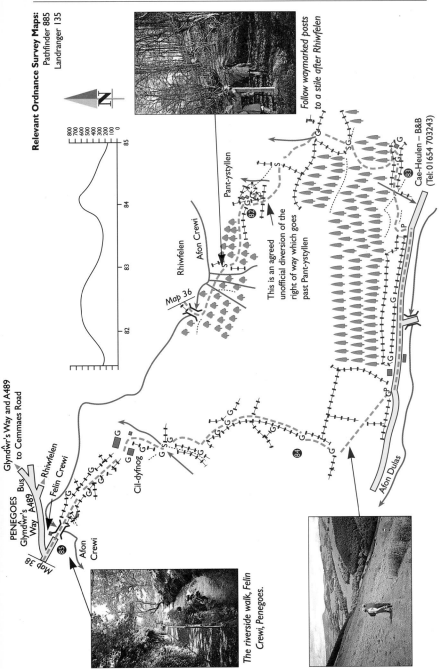

**Relevant Ordnance Survey Maps:**
Pathfinder 885
Landranger 135

*Follow waymarked posts to a stile after Rhiwfelen*

Cae-Heulen – B&B
(Tel: 01654 703243)

Pant-ystyllen

Rhiwfelen

Afon Crewi

Map 36

This is an agreed unofficial diversion of the right of way which goes past Pant-ystyllen

Afon Dulas

Cil-dyfnog

Glyndŵr's Way and A489 to Cemmaes Road

PENEGOES
Bus A489
Glyndŵr's Way
Felin Crewi
Rhiwfelen

Afon Crewi

Map 38

*The riverside walk, Felin Crewi, Penegoes.*

83

84

85

63

beyond the church. Was this, like the burial of Bran's head under the Tower of London, geomantic protection or rule after death? The head cult was deeply rooted in pagan Celtic practices (although Bran, whose story features in *The Mabinogion*, is credited with introducing Christianity to Britain). Detached heads were valued and venerated, evidently as links with the spirit world, and it can be reasonably assumed that in each case the spirit directly concerned was the former owner of the head. The church was founded by St Cadfarch, a descendant of Old King Cole, or Coel, in the mid-6th century, although the present building was erected in 1863. Across the old Roman road from the church are the holy wells or springs which are named after St Cadfarch, and which were lovingly restored by the Machynlleth & District Civic Society in 1984. Look for a slate step up from the road, near a tree which has a plaque fixed to it. If you suffer from rheumatism the water is reputed to bring relief! Penegoes is also the birthplace of the artist Richard Wilson, born in the Rectory in 1713. Wilson became a brilliant landscape painter whose paintings now hang in the National Gallery. He died at Mold in 1782.

The best way to appreciate Machynlleth's role as the market town of the Dyfi Valley is to come here on a Wednesday. To walk down Maengwyn Street is to enter a colourful, bustling street market which has endured since King Edward I granted the Lord of Powys a charter in 1291 to hold a market at Machynlleth for ever (plus two fairs a year). This charter was issued less than 10 years after Edward's conquest of Wales.

Machynlleth can lay claim to much more, however, for it was here that the great patriot Owain Glyndŵr was crowned before representatives from France, Scotland and Castile as the last native independent Prince of Wales. He held his first parliament in 1404 at a spot near the modern Mid Wales Tourist Information Centre. This excellent source of tourist information, which houses a display on the Dyfi Valley, is part of the Owain Glyndŵr Institute. The building on its left is the Parliament House. While the Tourist Information Centre is a mock late-medieval Welsh town house, the Parliament House, which houses an exhibition on Owain Glyndŵr, is genuinely old and may be the building that Glyndŵr used. It is at least in the right place. No wonder that when Jan Morris had a vision of a modern independent Wales in her book *The Matter of Wales*, she made Machynlleth its capital. Her President of the Republic lived in the mansion Plas Machynlleth, once the home of the Marquess of Londonderry. Lord Randolph Churchill (father of Sir Winston Churchill) was the nephew of the fifth marquess, Henry Vane-Tempest, and he visited frequently. Royalty also came here before the Plas and its grounds were presented to the town of Machynlleth after World War II. Your route passes the Londonderry family portrait gallery on the ground floor, before continuing past the children's playground.

# MACHYNLLETH

Train, bus, shops, cafes, ECD Thurs,
launderette, banks, post office, B&B
information from Tourist Information
Centre Tel: 01654 702401

Relevant Ordnance Survey Maps:
Pathfinder 885
Landranger 135
Grid Reference: SH 746008

Plas Machynlleth is now the home of
Celtica, the Welsh answer to York's Jorvik.
This unique attraction is open daily
Tel: 01654 702702.

Notice the horseshoe shaped door of an
old smithy just before you turn left from
Pentrerhedyn Street to Celtica.

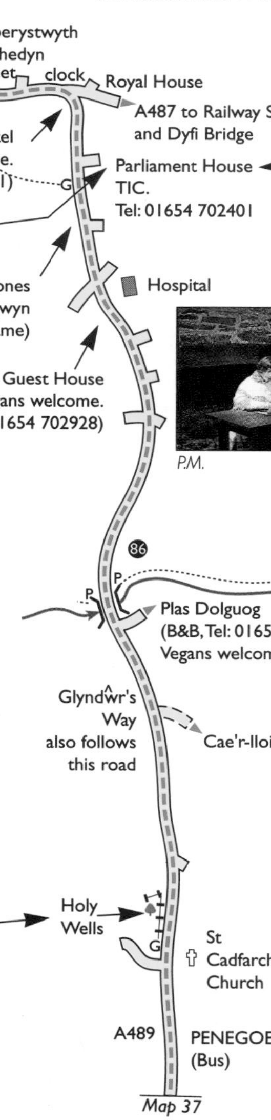

Notice a fine example of a timber-framed
house, dated 1628, on your left as you
walk down Maengwyn Street. Maengwyn
means white stone, referring to the white
stones outside Lo-Cost.

Plas Dolguog is a historic building that has been restored into a
very comfortable hotel, with a reputation for good food.
Dolguog means Cuog's Meadow, referring to Cuawg, son of
Cyndrwyn, Prince of part-Powys. Llywarch Hen, who is as
famous for his poetry as for his longevity, which spanned the late
5th century to the early 7th century, lived here as Cuawg's guest.
The present building dates from 1632 and was built by the
influential Herbert family. The rare Dolguog harebell flowers
here in July and August. It has tiny, pale blue bells and very small
pale green leaves, shaped like ivy.

*St Cadfarch's Holy Wells, Penegoes.*

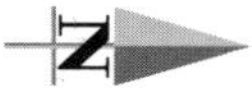

## Map labels

Celtica

A487 to Aberystwyth

Map 39

Pentrerhedyn
Street     clock

Royal House

A487 to Railway Station
and Dyfi Bridge

Wynnstay Arms Hotel
(B&B, Vegans welcome.
Tel: 01654 702941)

Parliament House
TIC.
Tel: 01654 702401

Owain
Glyndŵr
Centre

White Stones
(giving Maengwyn
Street its name)

Hospital

Maenllwyd Guest House
(B&B, Vegans welcome.
Tel: 01654 702928)

P.M.

Plas Dolguog
(B&B, Tel: 01654 702244).
Vegans welcome.

Afon
Dulas

Glyndŵr's
Way
also follows
this road

Cae'r-lloi

Holy
Wells

St
Cadfarch's
Church

A489

PENEGOES
(Bus)

Map 37

N.B. North is not at
the top of this map!

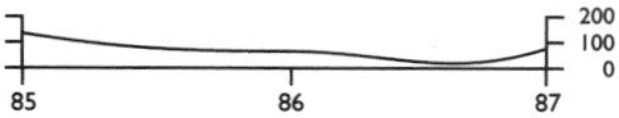

85     86     87

200
100
0

65

# Machynlleth - Furnace

## Section Eight (miles 87 - 96½)

The Roman Steps may indeed have been cut by the Romans. Machynlleth's own claim to fame as being the Roman Maglona has been disputed through lack of archaeological evidence, but the Roman fort at Pennal (Cefn Caer) probably did have a look-out post on this hill, Wylfa. The local mineral wealth was being exploited in Roman times and there may have been a track to the lead mines of Dylife.

The railway has been important to Machynlleth ever since its enthusiastic opening in January 1863, when 1500 passengers marched in procession to Machynlleth station for a special train, hauled by two locomotives, to Newtown and back. The right turn to the station at Machynlleth's Clock Tower makes a worthwhile diversion, taking you past the Royal House on your left and on to the Dyfi Bridge, uniting Powys and Gwynedd.

Dafydd Gam, who owed great personal loyalty to King Henry IV, attempted to assassinate Owain Glyndŵr in Machynlleth and was reputedly imprisoned in Royal House. Charles I is also connected with this very old building, although he probably failed to keep an appointment to sleep there in 1644. The distinctive Clock Tower was erected to mark the coming of age of Charles Stewart Vane-Tempest, Viscount Castlereagh, in 1873. Tourism is now one of the mainstays of the local economy and was given a boost when the Celtica exhibition, housed in the Plas, opened in 1995.

*The Afon Dyfi from the Dyfi Bridge, Machynlleth*

**Relevant Ordnance Survey Maps:**
Pathfinder 885
Outdoor Leisure 23
Landranger 135
Grid Reference: SH 746008

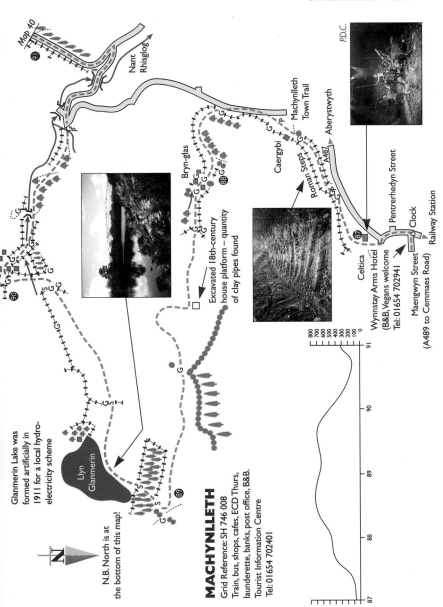

Map 40

91

Nant Rhisglog

Bryn-glas

88

Excavated 18th-century
house platform – quantity
of clay pipes found

90

Machynlleth
Town Trail

Caergybi

Roman Steps

A487

Aberystwyth

Pentrerhedyn Street

Clock

P.D.C.

87

Railway Station

Celtica

Wynnstay Arms Hotel
(B&B, Vegans welcome)
Tel: 01654 702941

Maengwyn Street
(A489 to Cemmaes Road)

Glanmerin Lake was
formed artificially in
1911 for a local hydro-
electricity scheme

Llyn
Glanmerin

89

N.B. North is at
the bottom of this map!

**MACHYNLLETH**
Grid Reference: SH 746 008
Train, bus, shops, cafes, ECD Thurs,
launderette, banks, post office, B&B.
Tourist Information Centre
Tel: 01654 702401

800
700
600
500
400
300
200
100
0

91

90

89

88

87

**Relevant Ordnance Survey Maps:**
Outdoor Leisure 23
Pathfinder 885
Landranger 135

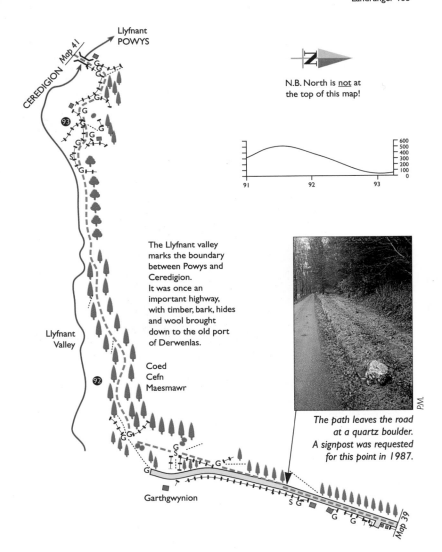

N.B. North is <u>not</u> at
the top of this map!

Llyfnant
POWYS

CEREDIGION

Map 41

93

Llyfnant
Valley

The Llyfnant valley
marks the boundary
between Powys and
Ceredigion.
It was once an
important highway,
with timber, bark, hides
and wool brought
down to the old port
of Derwenlas.

Coed
Cefn
Maesmawr

92

*The path leaves the road
at a quartz boulder.
A signpost was requested
for this point in 1987.*

Garthgwynion

Map 39

P.M.

**Relevant Ordnance Survey Maps:**
Outdoor Leisure 23
Landranger 135

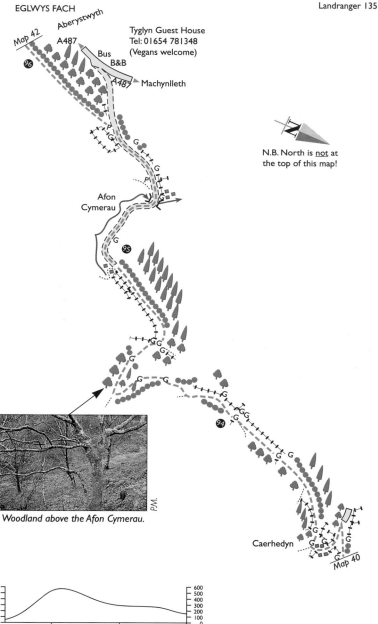

EGLWYS FACH

Aberystwyth

Map 42

A487

96

Tyglyn Guest House
Tel: 01654 781348
(Vegans welcome)

Bus
B&B

A487    Machynlleth

N.B. North is <u>not</u> at
the top of this map!

P

G

G

G

Afon
Cymerau

P

G

95

G

G

GG
G

G

G

G

94

GG
G

G

G G

Woodland above the Afon Cymerau.

P.M.

Caerhedyn

G

G
G

Map 40

600
500
400
300
200
100
0

94          95          96

Furnace derives its name from the disused, water-powered furnace which used to be part of an important ironworks. This has been restored and is now open to the public. The charcoal-burning blast furnace was built circa 1755, taking advantage of the charcoal provided by the local woodland. Its proximity to the coast allowed the easy use of imported iron ore from Cumbria. The water-wheel was used to power bellows which created the necessary draught for the very high temperatures needed to smelt iron. The furnace was abandoned in 1810 and was later converted into a sawmill. The nearby waterfall is in Cwm Einion, or Artists' Valley. It has attracted painters for over a century.

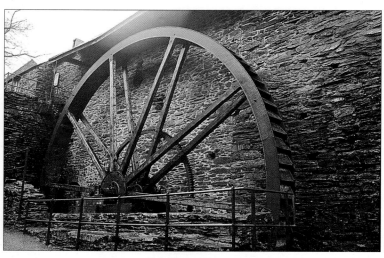

*The Millwheel, Furnace.*

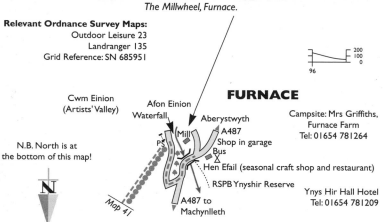

**Relevant Ordnance Survey Maps:**
Outdoor Leisure 23
Landranger 135
Grid Reference: SN 685951

Cwm Einion
(Artists' Valley)

N.B. North is at
the bottom of this map!

**N**

Afon Einion
Waterfall

Mill

P.S.

Map 41

**FURNACE**

Aberystwyth

A487

Shop in garage

Bus

Hen Efail (seasonal craft shop and restaurant)

RSPB Ynyshir Reserve

A487 to
Machynlleth

Campsite: Mrs Griffiths,
Furnace Farm
Tel: 01654 781264

Ynys Hir Hall Hotel
Tel: 01654 781209

# *Furnace - Borth*

The waterfall at Furnace.

**Relevant Ordnance Survey Maps:**
Outdoor Leisure 23
Landranger 135
Grid Reference: SN 685951

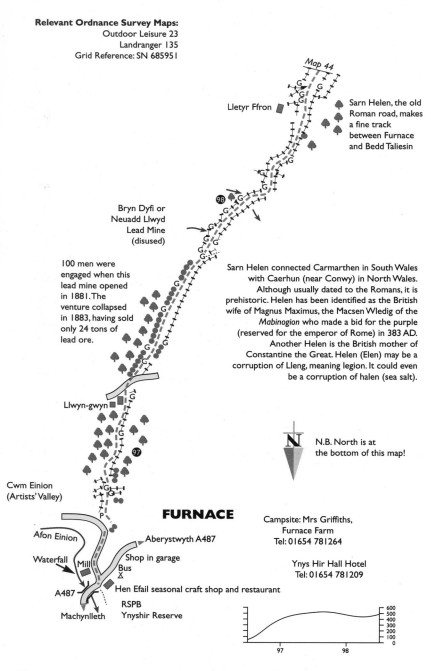

Map 44

Lletyr Ffron

Sarn Helen, the old Roman road, makes a fine track between Furnace and Bedd Taliesin

98

Bryn Dyfi or Neuadd Llwyd Lead Mine (disused)

100 men were engaged when this lead mine opened in 1881. The venture collapsed in 1883, having sold only 24 tons of lead ore.

Sarn Helen connected Carmarthen in South Wales with Caerhun (near Conwy) in North Wales. Although usually dated to the Romans, it is prehistoric. Helen has been identified as the British wife of Magnus Maximus, the Macsen Wledig of the *Mabinogion* who made a bid for the purple (reserved for the emperor of Rome) in 383 AD. Another Helen is the British mother of Constantine the Great. Helen (Elen) may be a corruption of Lleng, meaning legion. It could even be a corruption of halen (sea salt).

Llwyn-gwyn

97

N.B. North is at the bottom of this map!

Cwm Einion (Artists' Valley)

**FURNACE**

Afon Einion

Aberystwyth A487

Waterfall

Mill

Shop in garage
Bus

A487

Hen Efail seasonal craft shop and restaurant

Machynlleth

RSPB
Ynyshir Reserve

Campsite: Mrs Griffiths, Furnace Farm
Tel: 01654 781264

Ynys Hir Hall Hotel
Tel: 01654 781209

At last we have arrived, some 100 miles after setting out from Aberdyfi, at the reputed grave of the 6th century bard Taliesin, a contemporary of Myrddin (Merlin) and Arthur. Ranking with them in greatness, he was known as the "Chief of Bards".

Taliesin did live at the foot of this hill, so he could have been buried here. This round cairn with its cist grave dates from 2000 years before King Arthur fought the Saxons, however.

The tomb was disturbed in the 19th centrury, and it is said that when some people dug here they provoked thunder and lightning, causing them to flee.

A matter of a couple of thousand years may not concern us too much here. This is a very special place, linked by leys or spirit paths with others, including Carn March Arthur above Aberdyfi. Taliesin may be a title rather than a name. The stories told of him could be eternal.

Ceridwen, the great Celtic nature-goddess, gave birth to the ugly Afagddu. She determined to compensate him by brewing a concoction that would give him inspiration and knowledge. While she collected the necessary herbs at the correct astrological times, she set little Gwion, the son of the blacksmith of Llanfair Caereinion, to stir the brew for a year and a day. Gwion accidentally consumed the vital essence when he licked his fingers of three drops that contained the virtue of the brew. He fled from the vengeful Ceridwen and, after much shape-shifting, she swallowed Gwion and gave birth to him. Not having the heart now to kill him, she put the baby in a bag or coracle and floated him down the Dyfi, where he was found near Borth by Elphin, the son of Gwyddno Garanhir, at Beltane (May Day).

Elphin had been sent to catch fish at May Day as a test and he was jeered for being a poor fisherman. He named the baby Taliesin (Radiant Brow), however, and took him home with him. He soon made Elphin's court famous for bardism and the jealous Maelgwn Gwynedd had Elphin imprisoned at Deganwy, near Llandudno. Taliesin secured Elphin's release by winning a bardic contest with the Hanes Taliesin, which included such lines as *Johannes the Diviner I was called by Myrddin, Now every king shall call me Taliesin*. This could refer to the natural, unregenerate man being born again as the raised-up perfected man.

> *Their Lord they shall praise,*
> *Their language they shall keep,*
> *Their land they shall lose*
> *Except Wild Wales.*

Taliesin: *Destiny of the Britons*

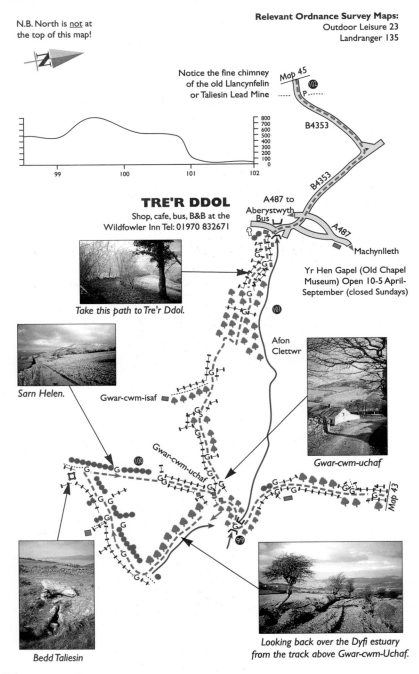

N.B. North is <u>not</u> at the top of this map!

**Relevant Ordnance Survey Maps:**
Outdoor Leisure 23
Landranger 135

Notice the fine chimney of the old Llancynfelin or Taliesin Lead Mine

Map 45

P

B4353

B4353

## TRE'R DDOL
Shop, cafe, bus, B&B at the Wildfowler Inn Tel: 01970 832671

A487 to Aberystwyth
Bus

A487

Machynlleth

Yr Hen Gapel (Old Chapel Museum) Open 10-5 April-September (closed Sundays)

*Take this path to Tre'r Ddol.*

Afon Clettwr

*Sarn Helen.*

Gwar-cwm-isaf

Gwar-cwm-uchaf

*Gwar-cwm-uchaf*

Map 43

*Looking back over the Dyfi estuary from the track above Gwar-cwm-Uchaf.*

*Bedd Taliesin*

**Relevant Ordnance Survey Maps:**
Outdoor Leisure 23
Landranger 135

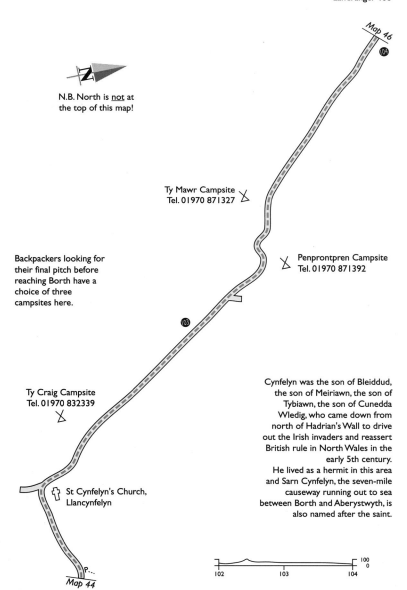

N.B. North is <u>not</u> at
the top of this map!

Ty Mawr Campsite
Tel. 01970 871327

Backpackers looking for
their final pitch before
reaching Borth have a
choice of three
campsites here.

Penprontpren Campsite
Tel. 01970 871392

Ty Craig Campsite
Tel. 01970 832339

Cynfelyn was the son of Bleiddud,
the son of Meiriawn, the son of
Tybiawn, the son of Cunedda
Wledig, who came down from
north of Hadrian's Wall to drive
out the Irish invaders and reassert
British rule in North Wales in the
early 5th century.
He lived as a hermit in this area
and Sarn Cynfelyn, the seven-mile
causeway running out to sea
between Borth and Aberystwyth, is
also named after the saint.

St Cynfelyn's Church,
Llancynfelyn

*Map 44*

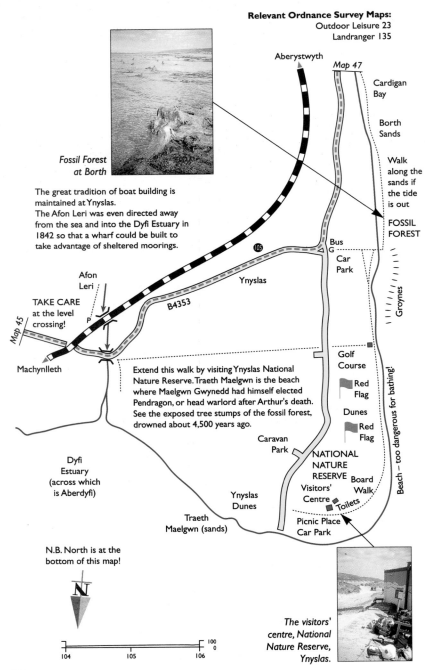

**Relevant Ordnance Survey Maps:**
Outdoor Leisure 23
Landranger 135

Aberystwyth

Map 47

Cardigan Bay

Borth Sands

Walk along the sands if the tide is out

FOSSIL FOREST

*Fossil Forest at Borth*

The great tradition of boat building is maintained at Ynyslas.
The Afon Leri was even directed away from the sea and into the Dyfi Estuary in 1842 so that a wharf could be built to take advantage of sheltered moorings.

Bus

Car Park

Groynes

Afon Leri

Ynyslas

B4353

TAKE CARE at the level crossing!

Map 45

P

Machynlleth

Golf Course

Red Flag

Dunes

Red Flag

Beach – too dangerous for bathing!

Extend this walk by visiting Ynyslas National Nature Reserve. Traeth Maelgwn is the beach where Maelgwn Gwynedd had himself elected Pendragon, or head warlord after Arthur's death. See the exposed tree stumps of the fossil forest, drowned about 4,500 years ago.

Caravan Park

NATIONAL NATURE RESERVE

Board Walk

Visitors' Centre

Toilets

Dyfi Estuary (across which is Aberdyfi)

Ynyslas Dunes

Picnic Place Car Park

Traeth Maelgwn (sands)

N.B. North is at the bottom of this map!

**N**

100
0

104          105          106

*The visitors' centre, National Nature Reserve, Ynyslas.*

**Relevant Ordnance Survey Maps:**
Outdoor Leisure 23
Either Pathfinder 926 or Pathfinder 927
Landranger 135
Grid Reference: SN 609901

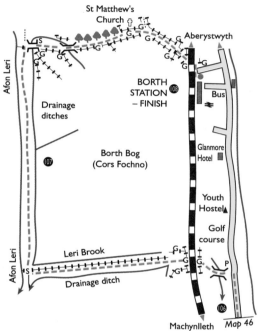

# BORTH

Train, bus, shops, post office, bank, launderette, cafe, ECD Wed, B&B including Glanmore Hotel Tel: 01970 871689 and Borth Youth Hostel Tel: 01970 871498. TIC. Tel: 01970 871174.

Borth is built on a long narrow, shingle bank which the sea flows under to the bogland behind. Easy access to a fine four-mile-long beach has made Borth a popular resort, served by the railway since 1863.

N.B. North is at
the bottom of this map!

| 106 | 107 | 108 |

P.M.

*The sunset over Borth Sands. The end of your 108-mile journey.*

# Walking the Way – transport and accommodation

If you are a diehard backpacker and long-distance walker you can skip this page. All you need to know is that you can take a train to the start at Aberdyfi and from the finish at Borth, and that there are campsites or other means of accommodation at reasonable intervals for a day's walk, as indicated on the mileage and facilities chart and detailed at the appropriate places on the strip map. This little extra is for ordinary mortals who fear for their comfort.

Public transport is not what you may be used to in other parts of Britain, but it does exist and you can divide this route into short sections with its aid. As well as trains, there are buses run by Crosville Cymru. Full details are available from Crosville Wales Ltd, Imperial Buildings, Glan-y-Mor Road, Llandudno Junction, LL31 9RH, Tel. 01492 592111. Their district office is at Park Avenue, Aberystwyth, Tel. 01970 617951. Gwynedd County Council produce an excellent timetable, available for an A5 sae from local Tourist Information Centres or from the County Offices, Caernarfon, Gwynedd, LL55 ISH, Tel. 01286 679535. Send an A5 sae for a free map and timetable, too, to Powys County Council, County Hall, Llandrindod, LDI 5LG, Tel. 01597 826643.

It is possible to base yourself at, say, Machynlleth and walk the Dyfi Valley Way in a series of day trips. A local taxi might prove convenient in places. It's easier during term-time when the school buses run to Dinas Mawddwy from both Machynlleth and Dolgellau (connections for Llanuwchllyn).

To gain a real sense of pilgrimage, do try to complete this route in one trip, either carrying a tent or by staying in B&Bs, carrying very little. Awake each morning with a new destination ahead of you.

## Suggested trip

| | |
|---|---|
| **Saturday** | Arrive in Aberdyfi. Walk to Pennal (B&B). |
| **Sunday** | Walk to Pantperthog (camping) or Corris (B&B), making visit to the Centre for Alternative Technology. |
| **Monday** | Visit King Arthur's Labyrinth before walking to Dinas Mawddwy (camping and B&B). |
| **Tuesday** | Walk to Llanuwchllyn (B&B – leave tent in Dinas Mawddwy) |
| **Wednesday** | Walk to Dinas Mawddwy (B&B or return to tent). |
| **Thursday** | Walk to Darowen (B&B or camping). |
| **Friday** | Walk to Machynlleth (B&B), visiting Felin Crewi, Canolfan Owain Glyndŵr and Celtica. |
| **Saturday** | Walk to Furnace (camping or B&B at Eglwys Fach), visit RSPB, Ynyshir. |
| **Sunday** | Walk to Borth for train home or stay (camping, B&B). |

Walking boots will help you enjoy this walk, while an anorak should keep out any wind and rain. Emergency rations of food and drink can be carried in a lightweight rucksack. Refreshments are often available along the way and this information is given.

Visiting ancient sites makes a subscription to CADW (Welsh Historic Monuments) a worthwhile proposition. Full details are available from CADW, Brunel House, 2 Fitzalan Road, Cardiff CF2 1UY (Tel: 01222 500200).

As you wander around the principality, the services of the Wales Tourist Board will prove invaluable. Contact the Wales Tourist Board at Brunel House, 2 Fitzalan Road, Cardiff CF2 1UY (Tel: 01222 499909).

Help preserve our network of public footpaths and bridleways and enjoy them in the company of others by joining the Ramblers' Association. Contact the Ramblers' Association, Ty'r Cerddwyr, High Street, Gresford, Wrexham, Clwyd LL12 8PT (Tel: 01978 855148).

If you aren't a member of the Youth Hostels Association but would like to use their hostels at Corris, Bala or Borth, you can obtain membership details from the YHA, Trevelyan House, 8 St Stephen's Hill, St Albans, Herts AL1 2DY. Tel: 01727 855215.

If you are camping, invaluable help (including the best sites guide and map) comes with membership of the Camping & Caravanning Club, Greenfields House, Westwood Way, Coventry CV4 8JH. Tel: 01203 694995.

## Remember the Country Code!

Enjoy the countryside and respect it.
Guard against all risk of fire.
Leave gates as you find them.
Keep your dogs under close control.
Keep to public paths across famland.
Use gates and stiles to cross fences, hedges and walls.
Leave livestock, crops and machinery alone.
Take your litter home.
Help to keep all water clean.
Protect wildlife, plants and trees.
Take special care on country roads.
Make no unnecessary noise.

Please use this page to make any notes about the walk that you may like to keep.
This will help you keep your map pages free from unsightly pen marks.

# Key to Maps

| | |
|---|---|
| ----○⑩--- | The footpath route, with distance walked from the start in miles |
| ............. | Other paths |
| ⬭⬭⬭ | Motor roads |
| ⊏⊏⊏⊏⊏ | Partly-metalled lanes |
| ▬▬▬ | Railway line |
| ⊢⊢⊢⊢⊢⊢ | Hedge or fence |
| ●●●●●●●● | Wall |
| ∞ | Standing stones |
| ▣ | Cairn, mound |
| G | Gate |
| S | Stile |
| P | Signpost |
| ⟶ | Stream or river, with direction of flow |
| ⫯⫯⟶ | Bridge |
| △ | Peak |
| ﹨﹨ⁱⁱⁱ∕∕ | Steep, dangerous, crags |
| 🌲🌳 | Trees |
| ▬ ▮ | Buildings |
| ▭ | Ruin |
| ✟ | Church or chapel |
| ▲ | Youth hostel |
| ✕ | Camp site |
| ⵣ | Windmill |
| T | Telephone box (selected ones only) |
| ⇌ | Railway station |
| ⊢N▶ | Direction of north |

0 |_____ Scale: one mile _____| 

Each map has a gradient profile showing the height in feet above sea level and the distance in miles from the start.

Afon is Welsh for river, nant means stream.